FEATHERS
AN ADULT COLORING BOOK

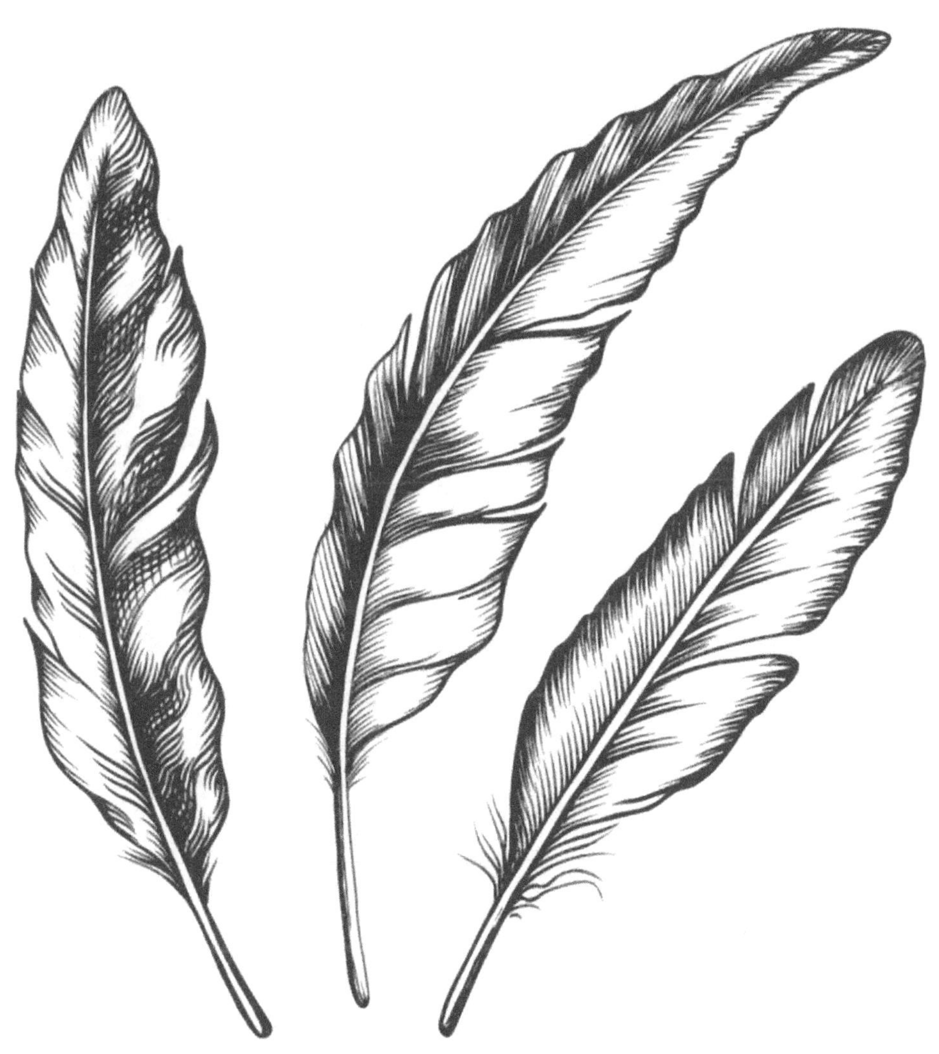

52 Feather Coloring Pages

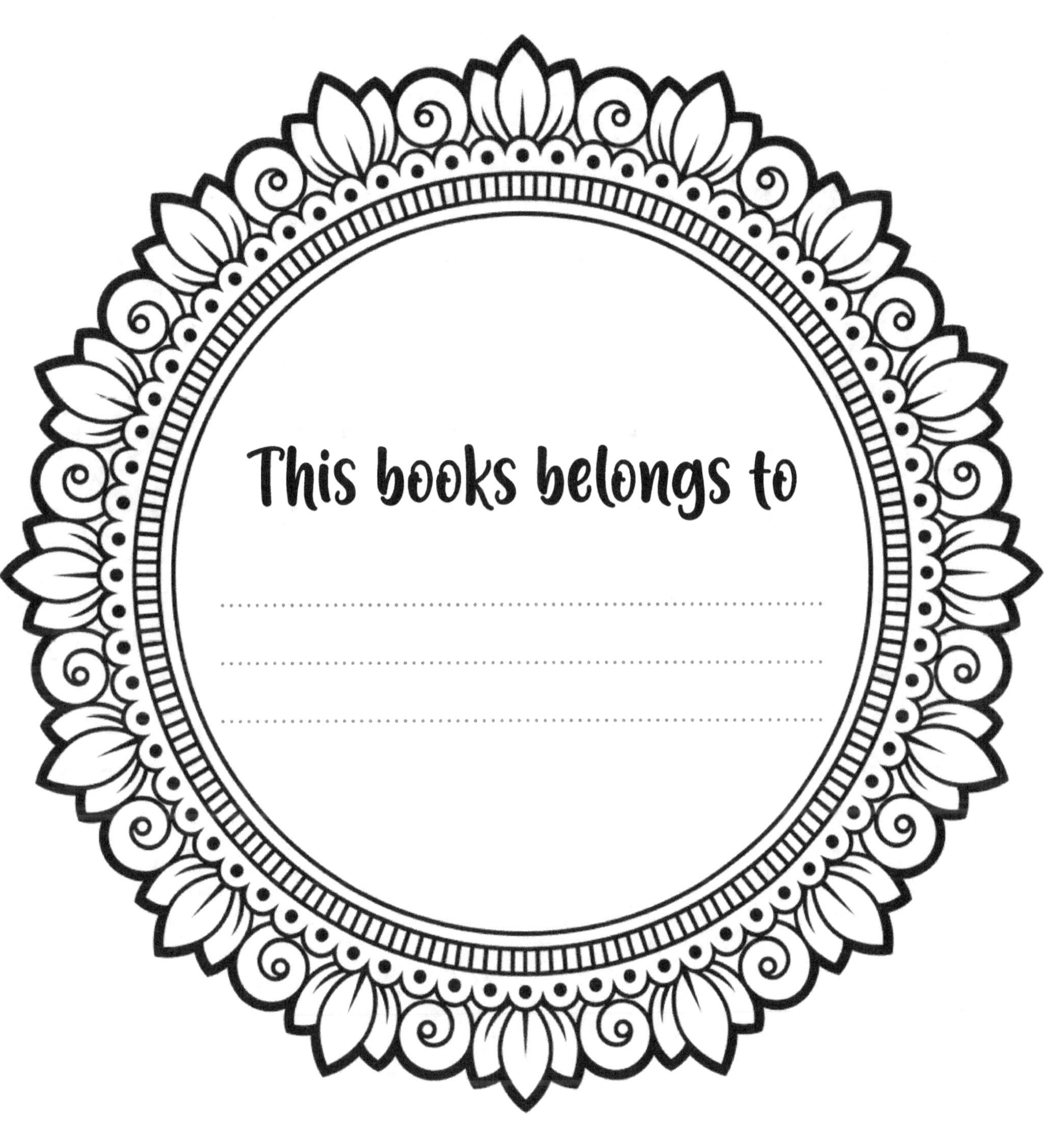

This books belongs to

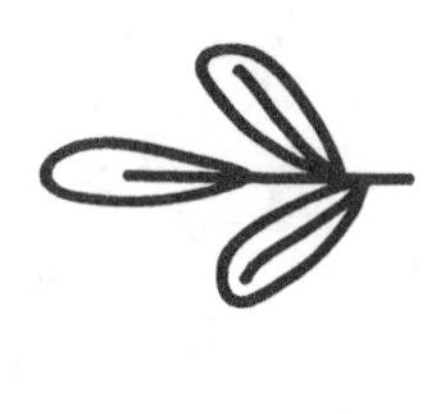 Color Test Page 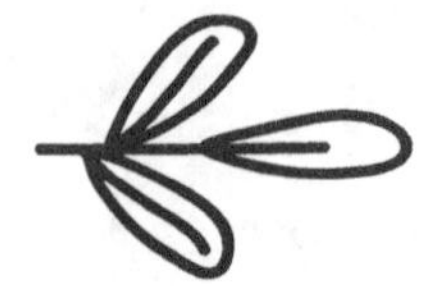

 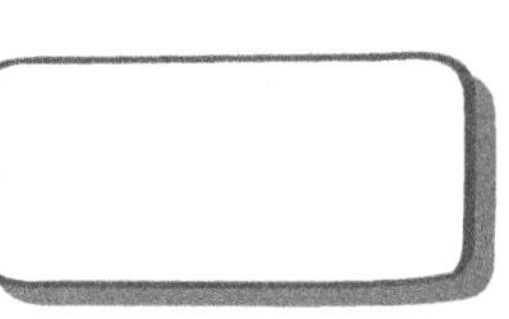 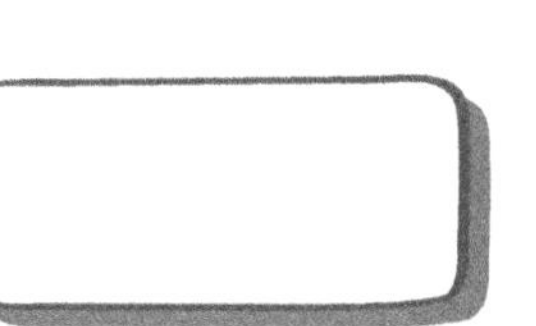 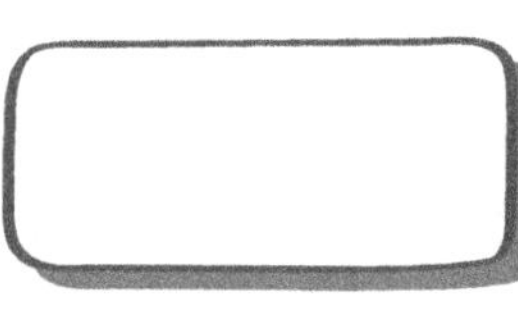

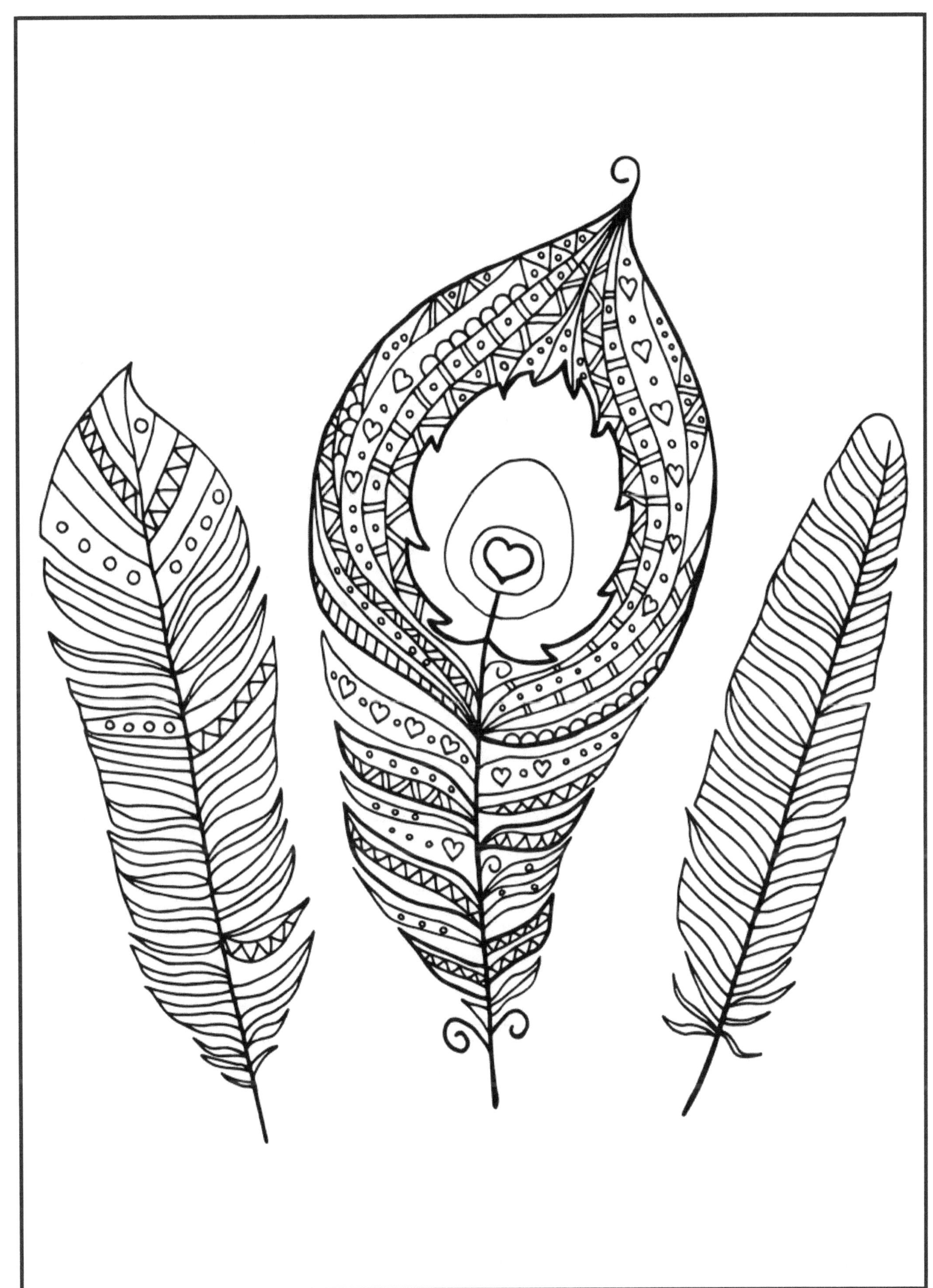

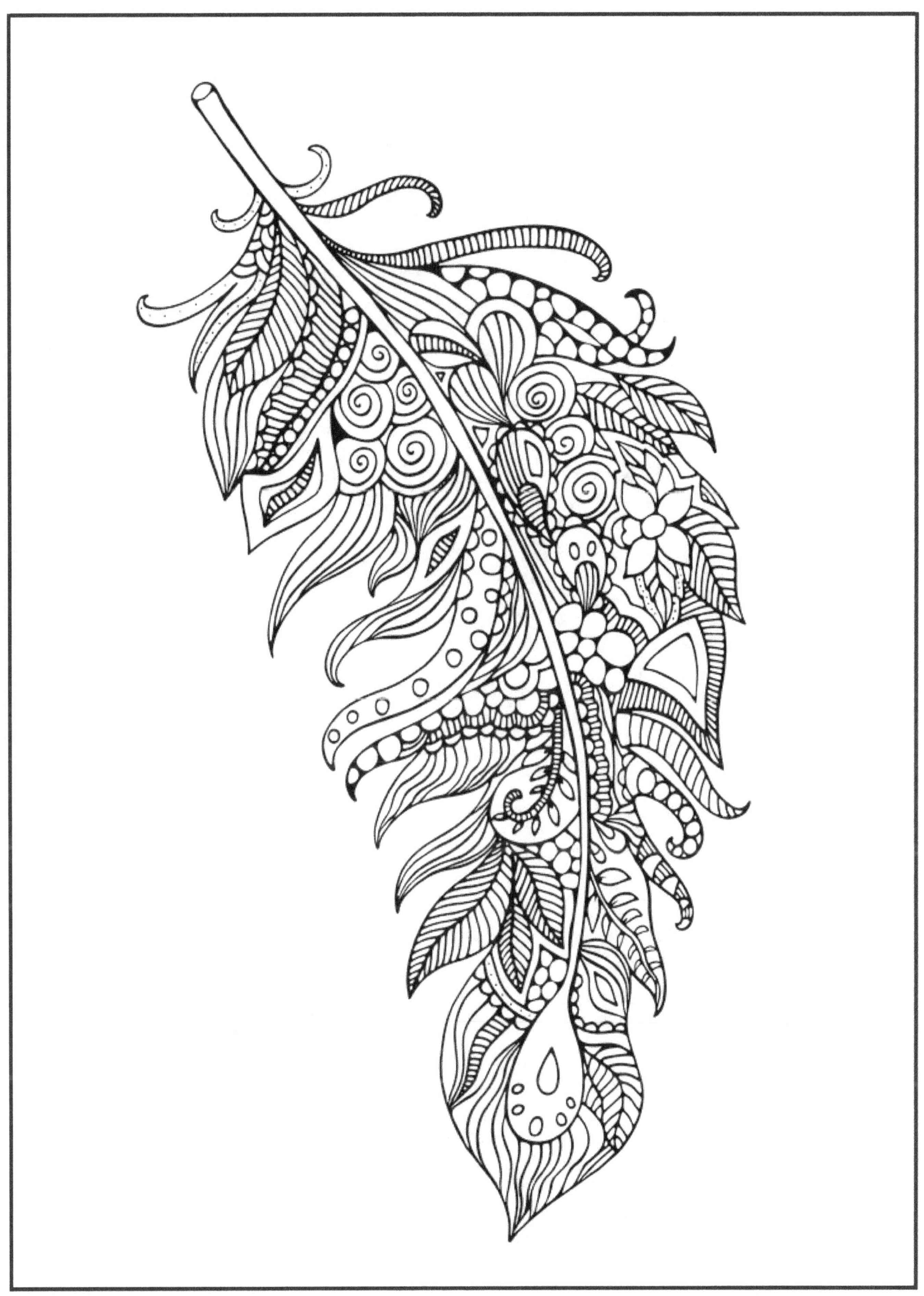

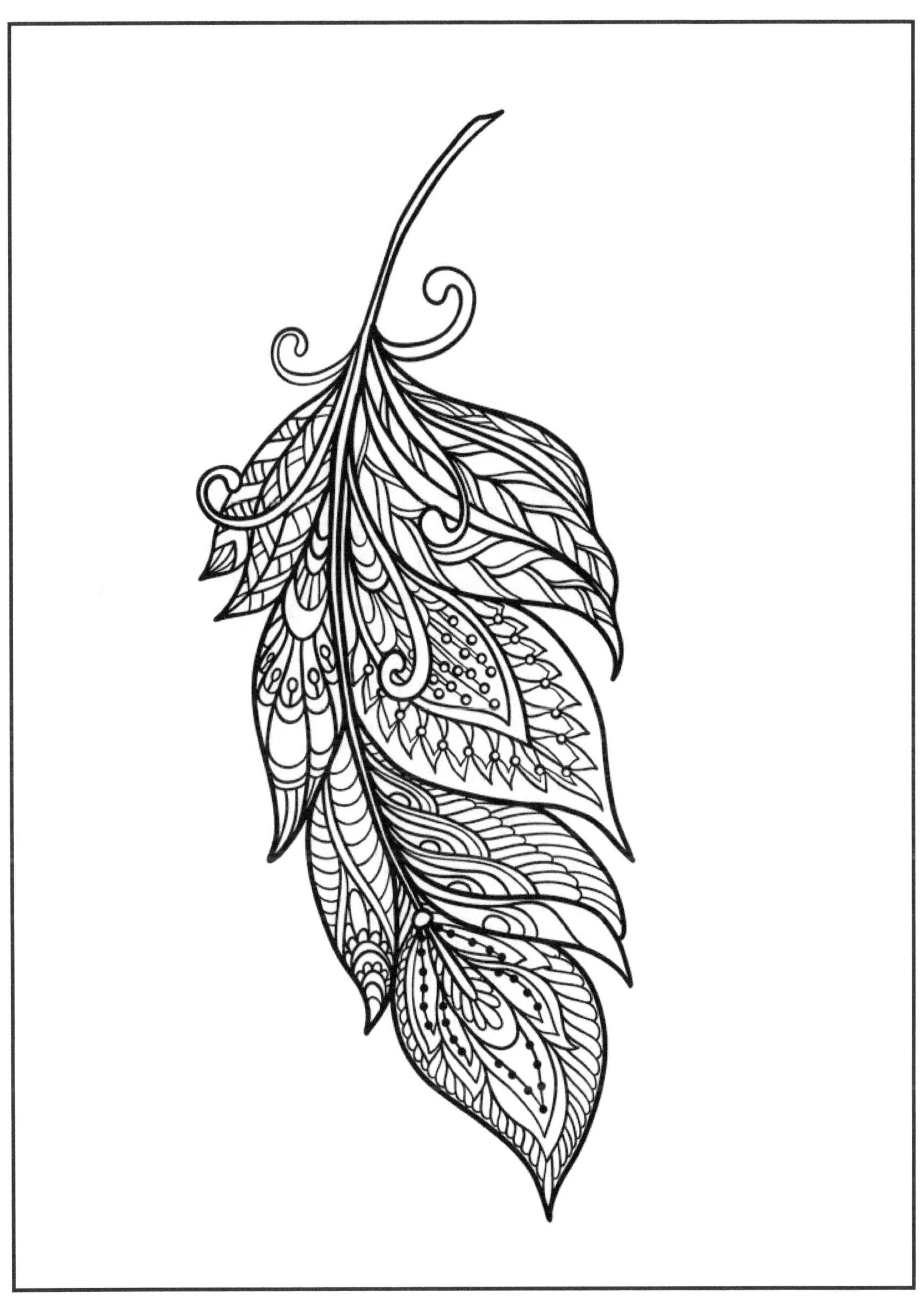

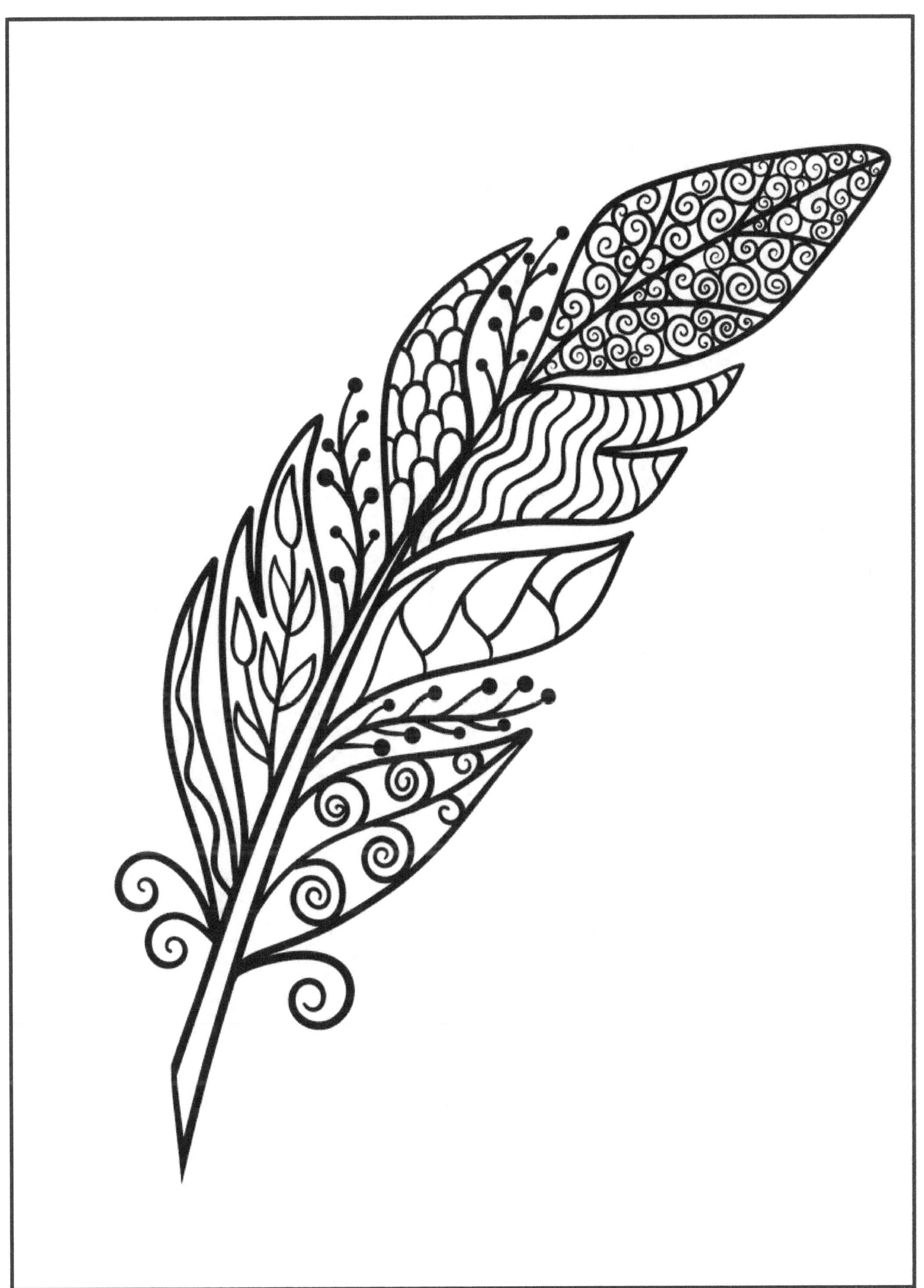

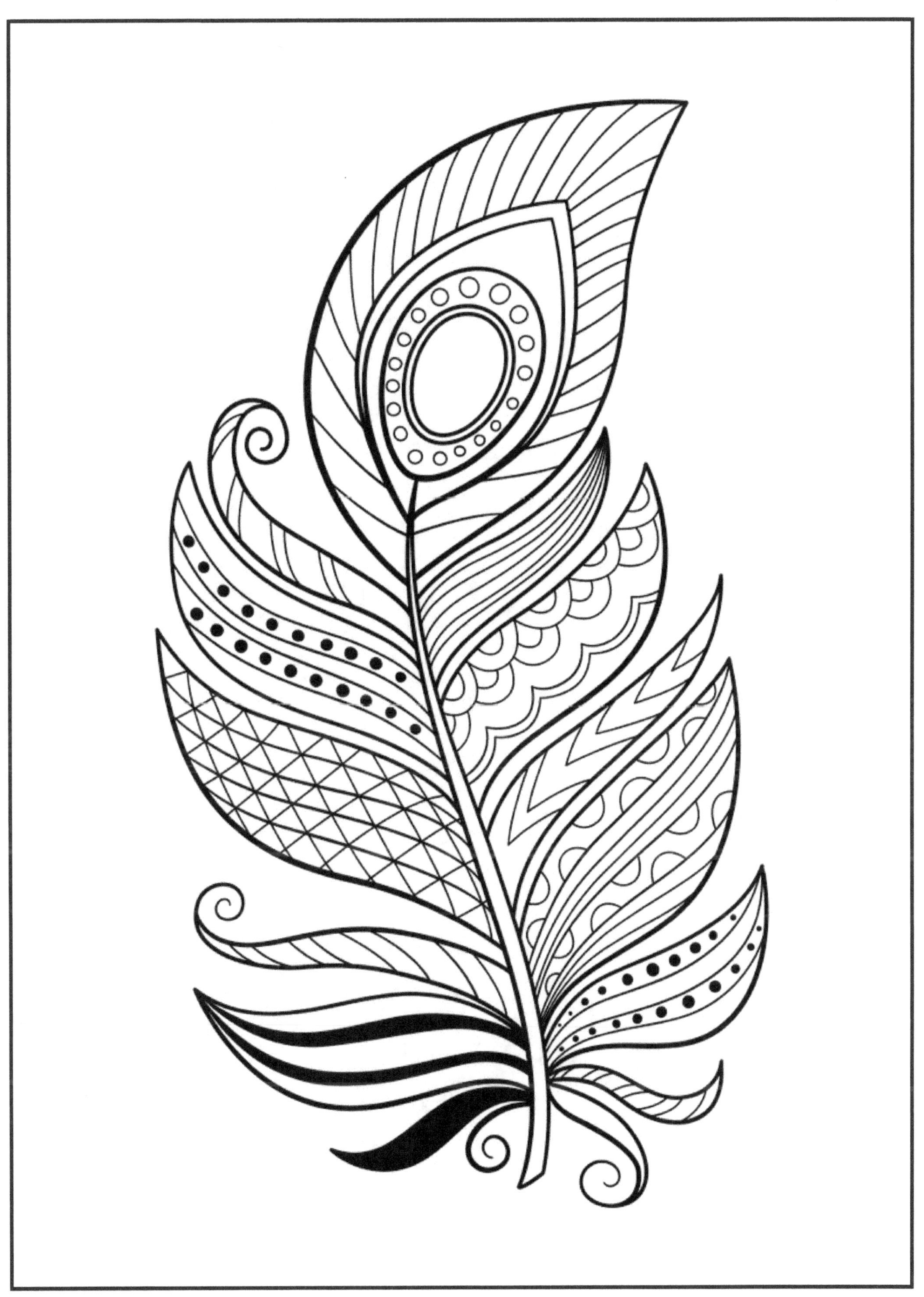

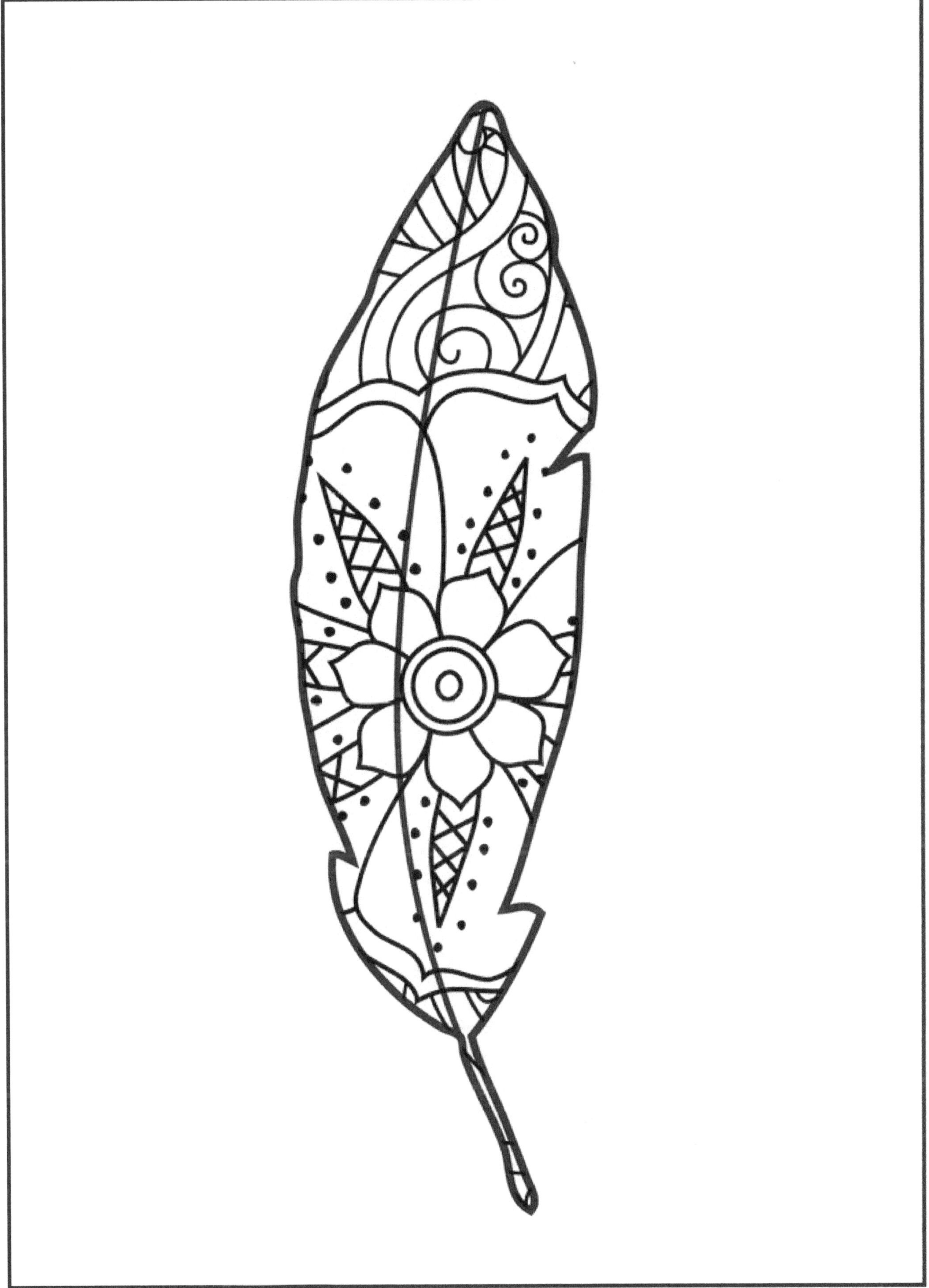

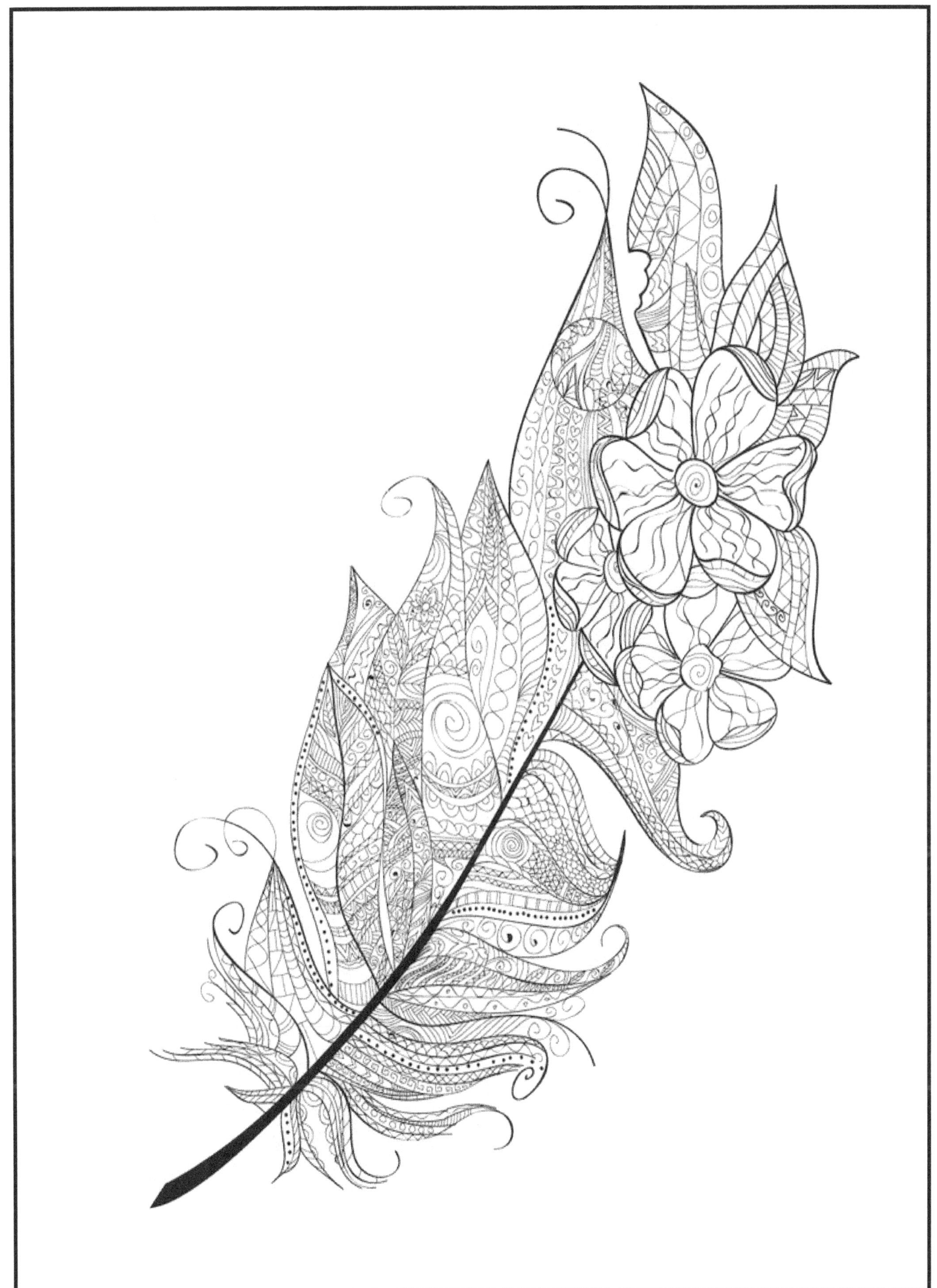

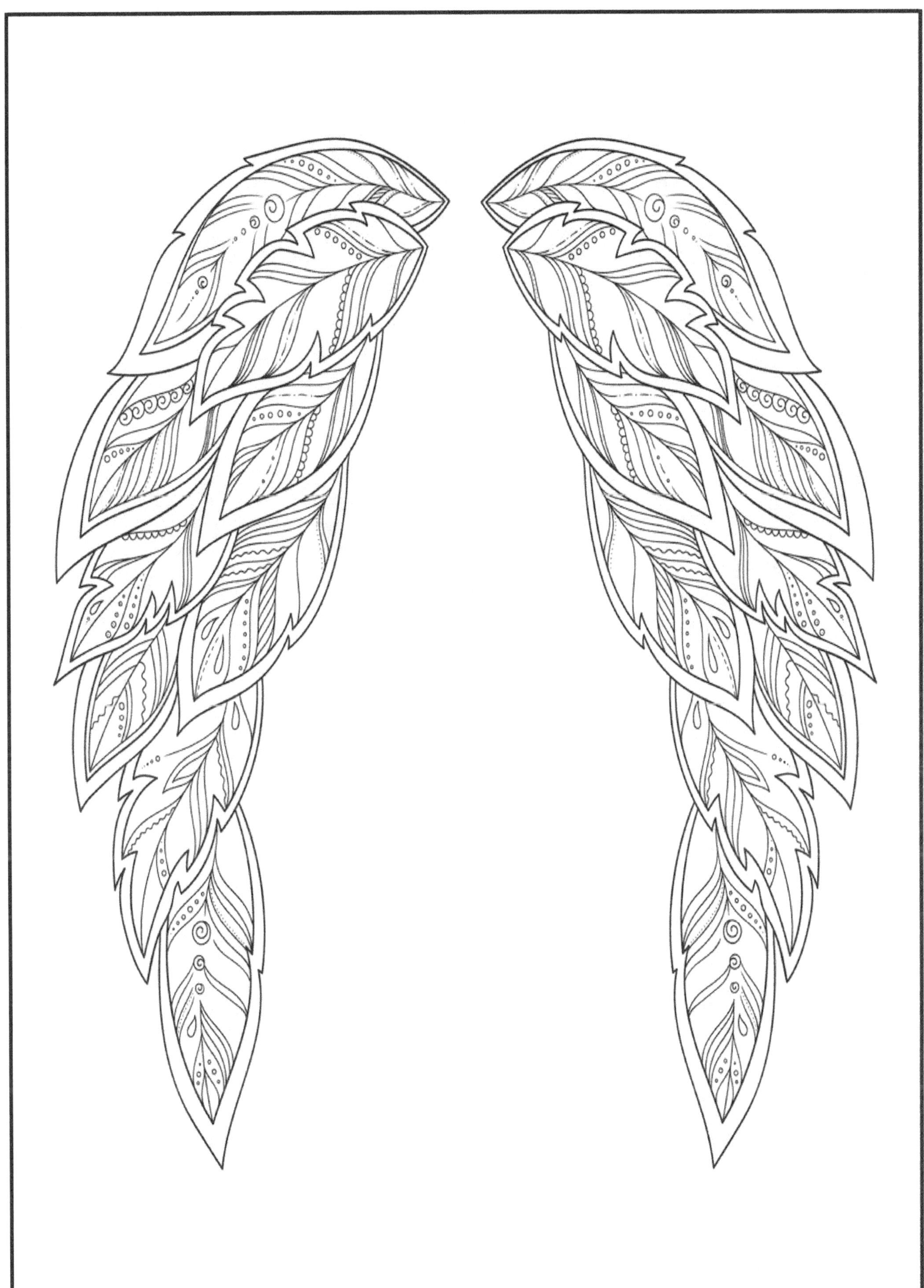

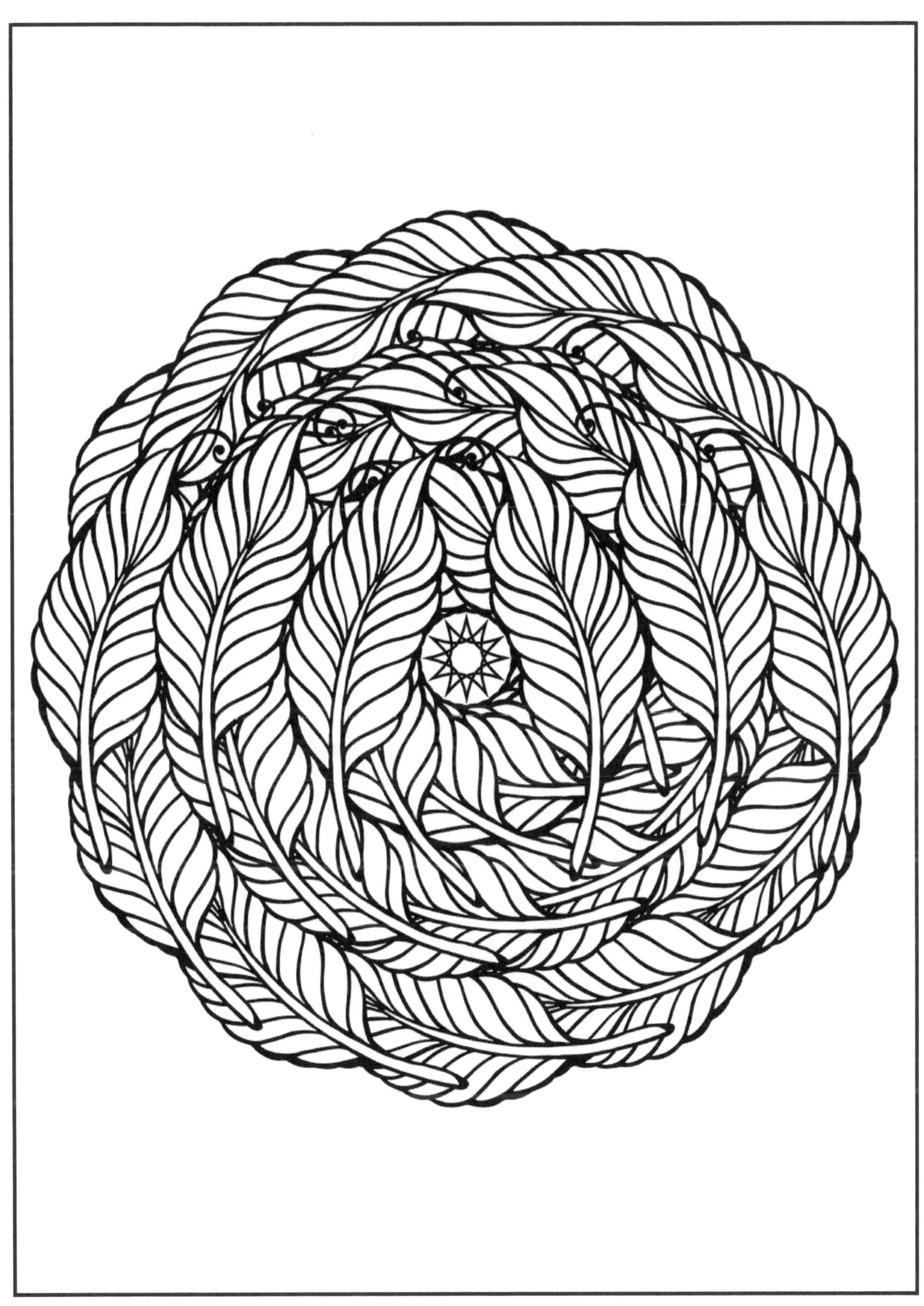

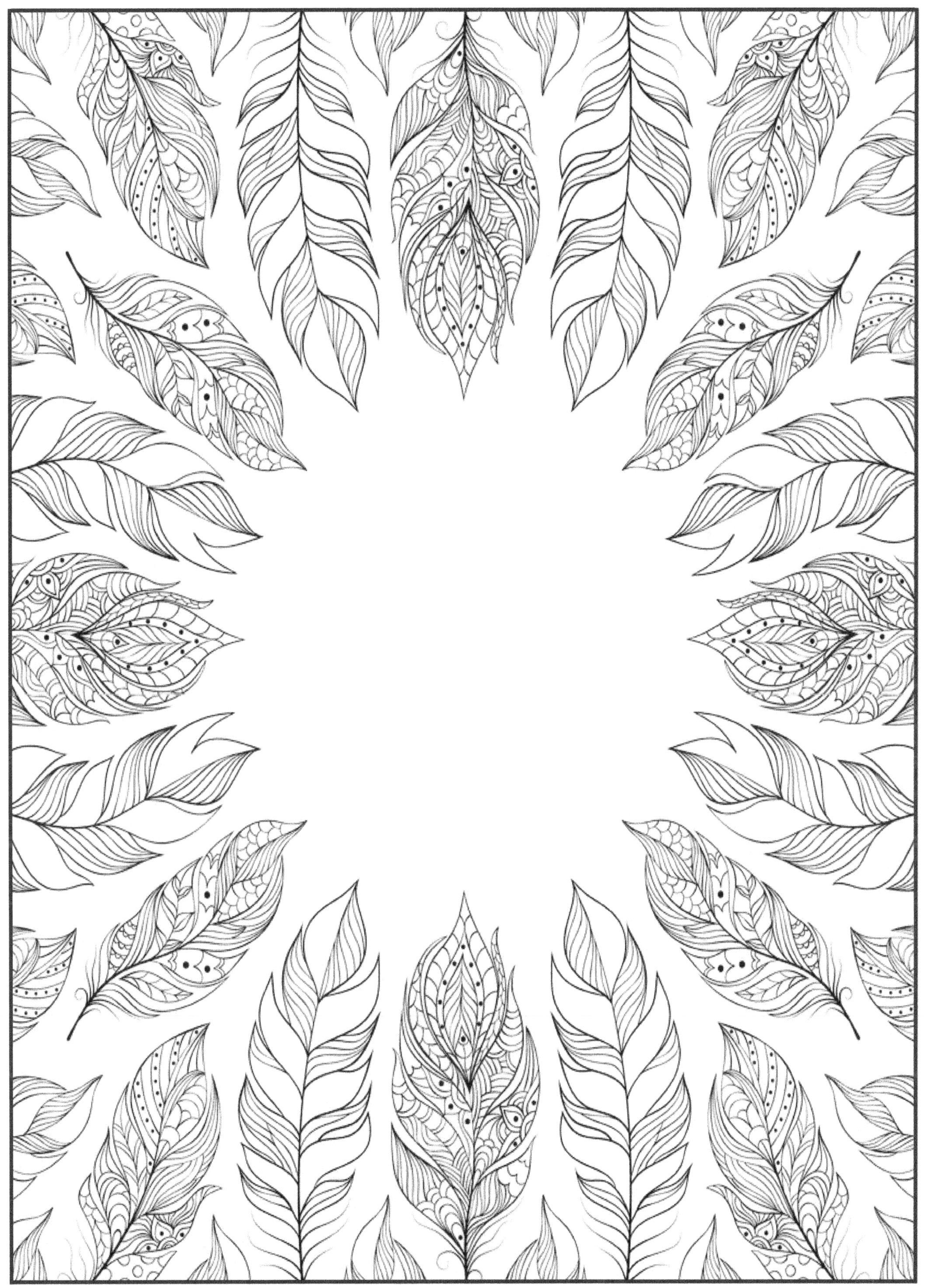

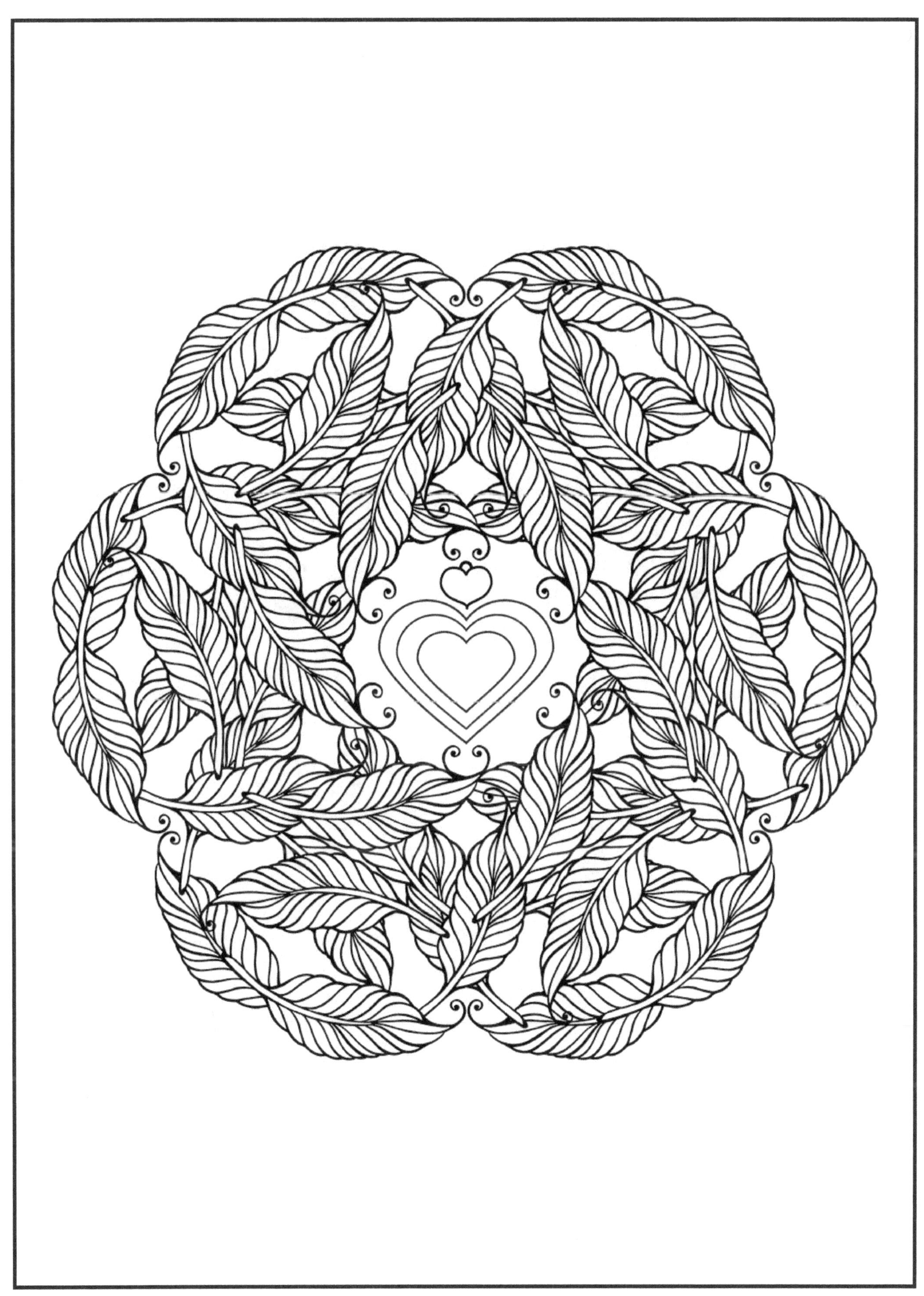

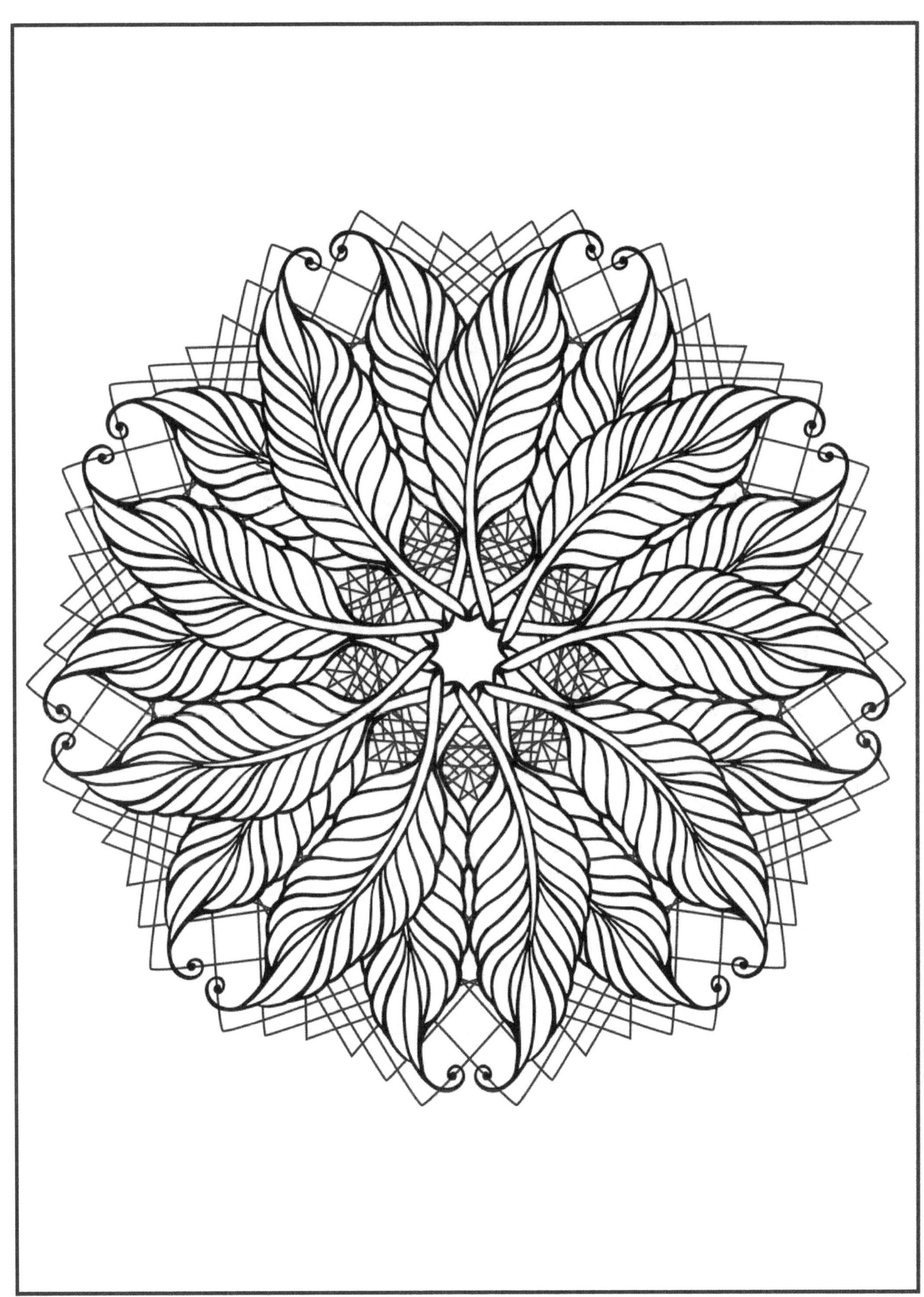

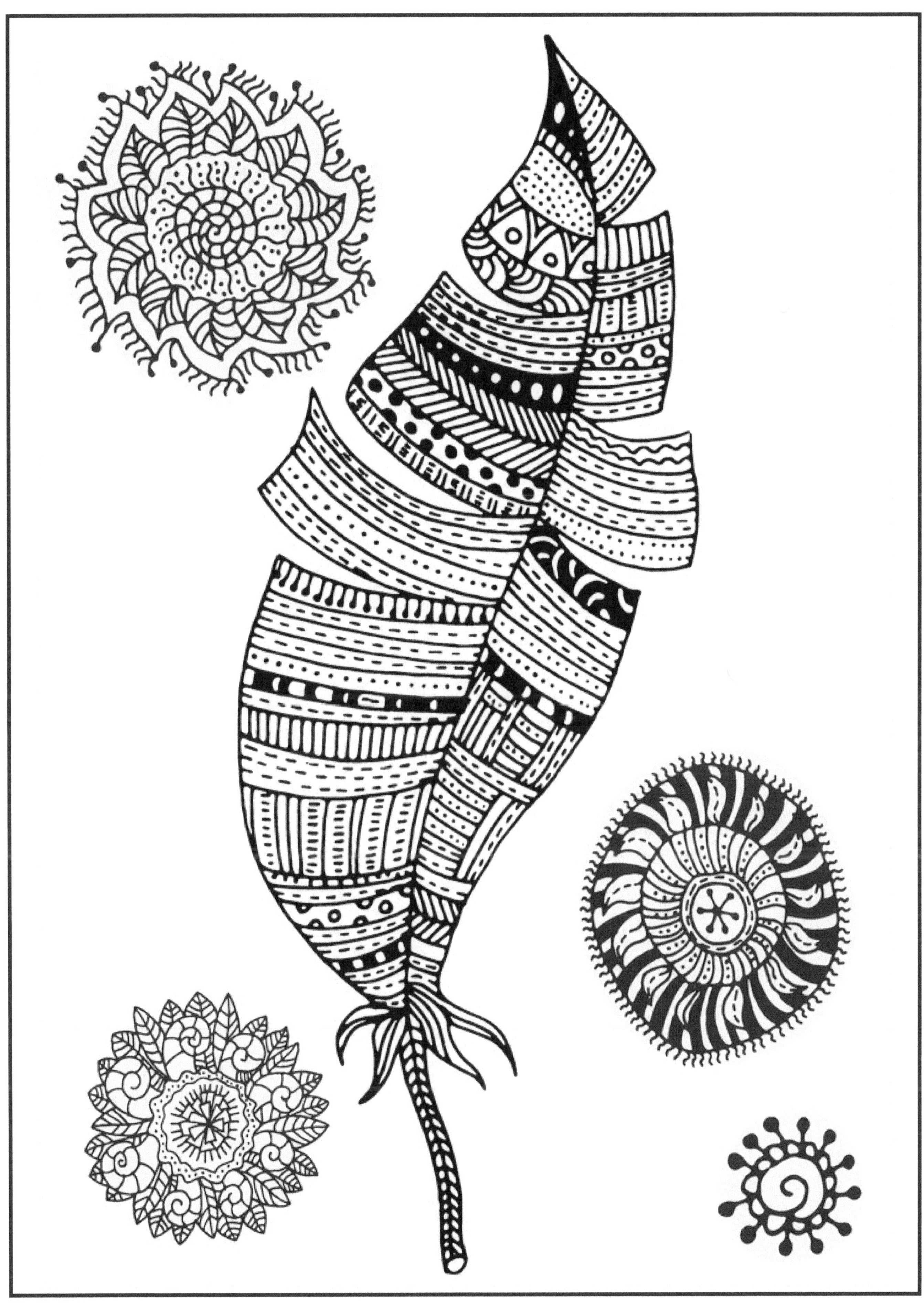

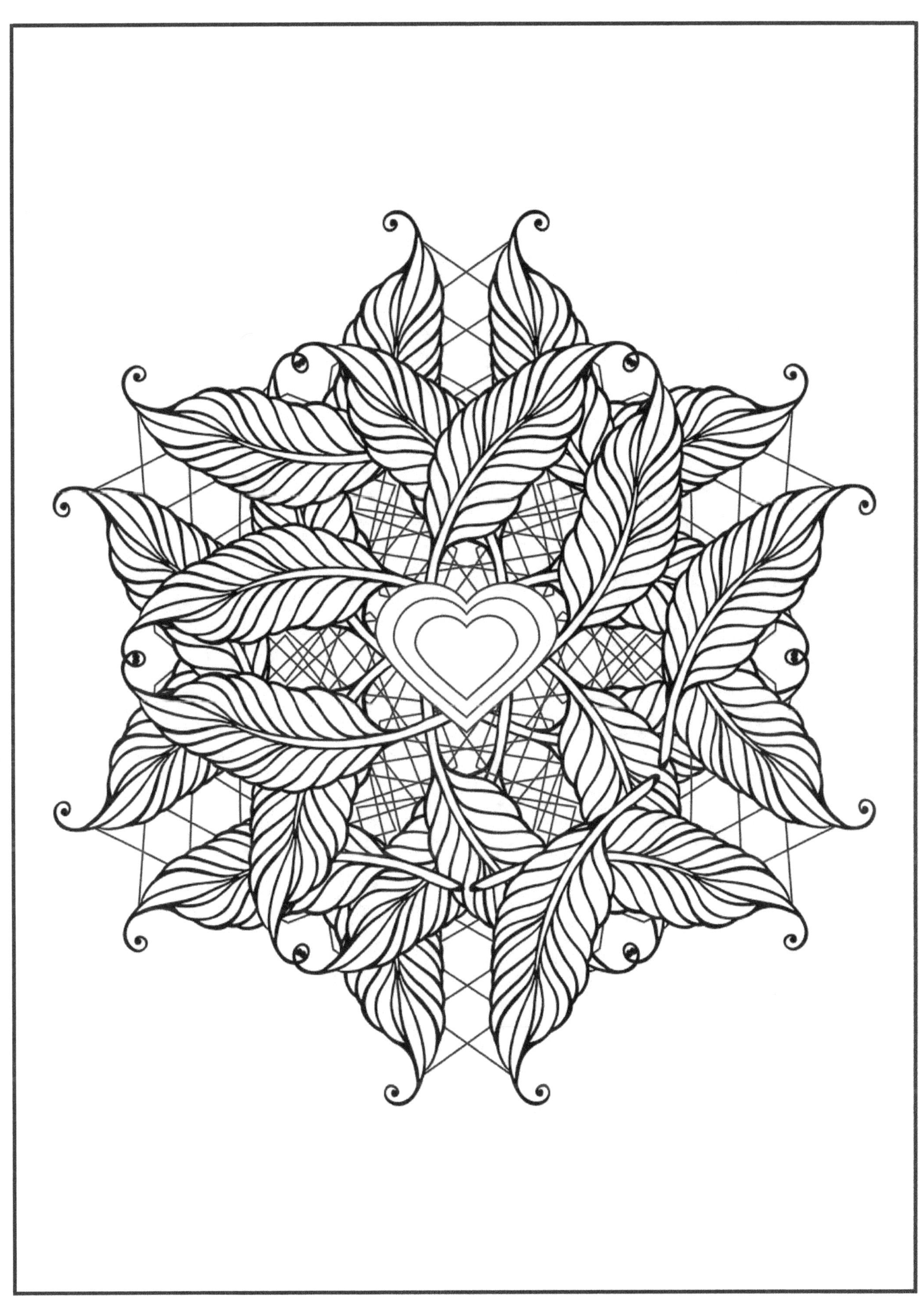

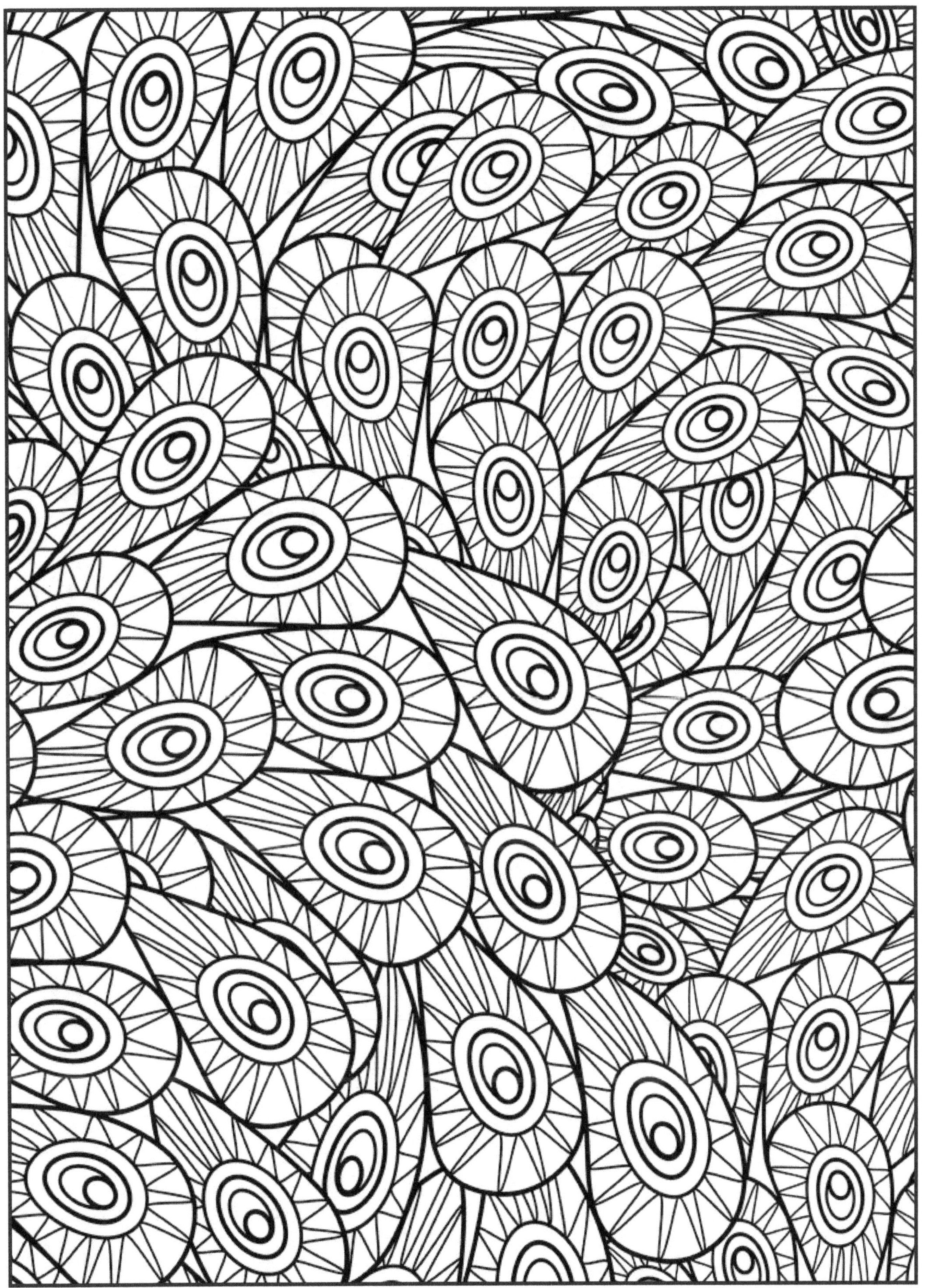

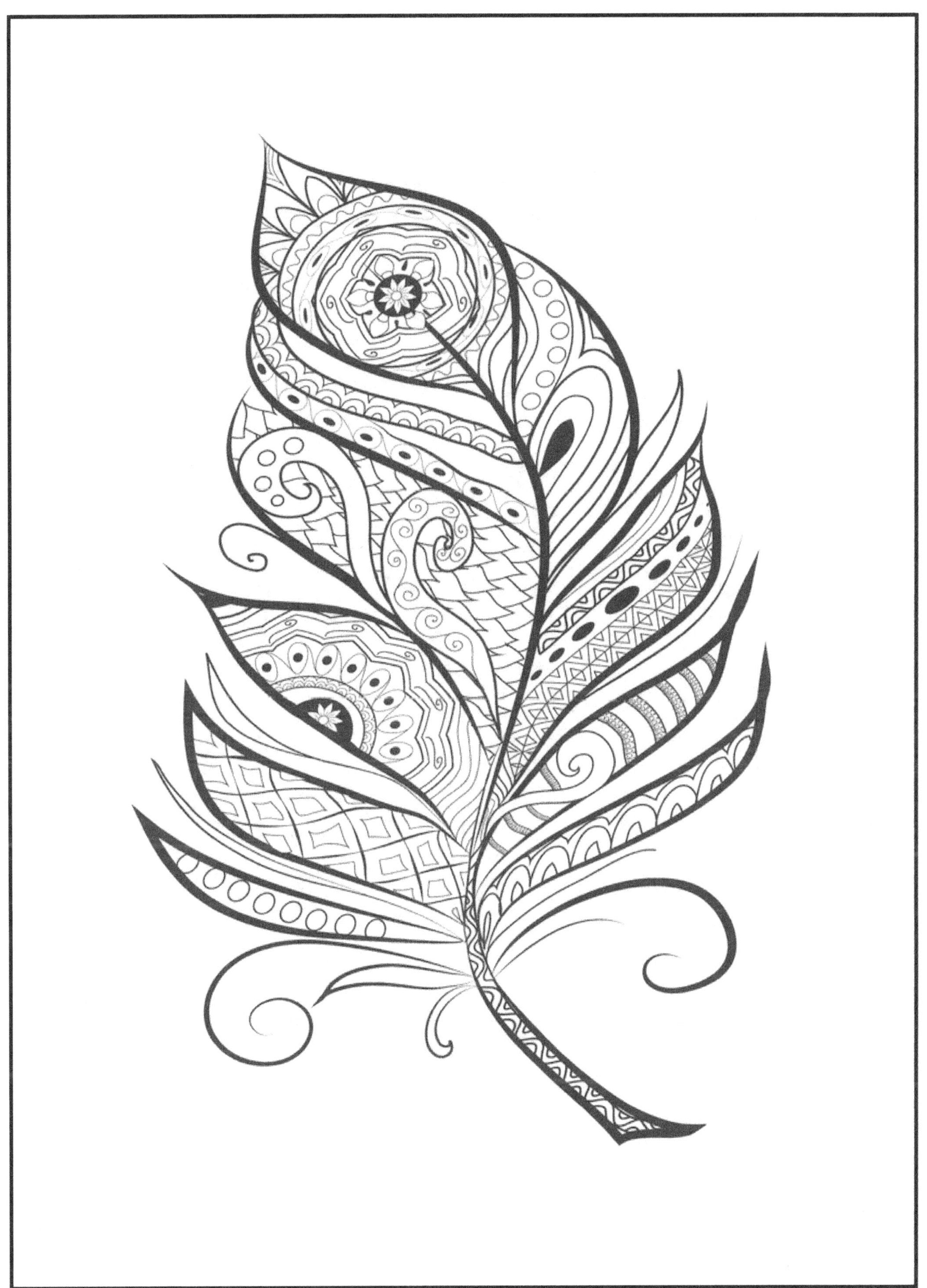

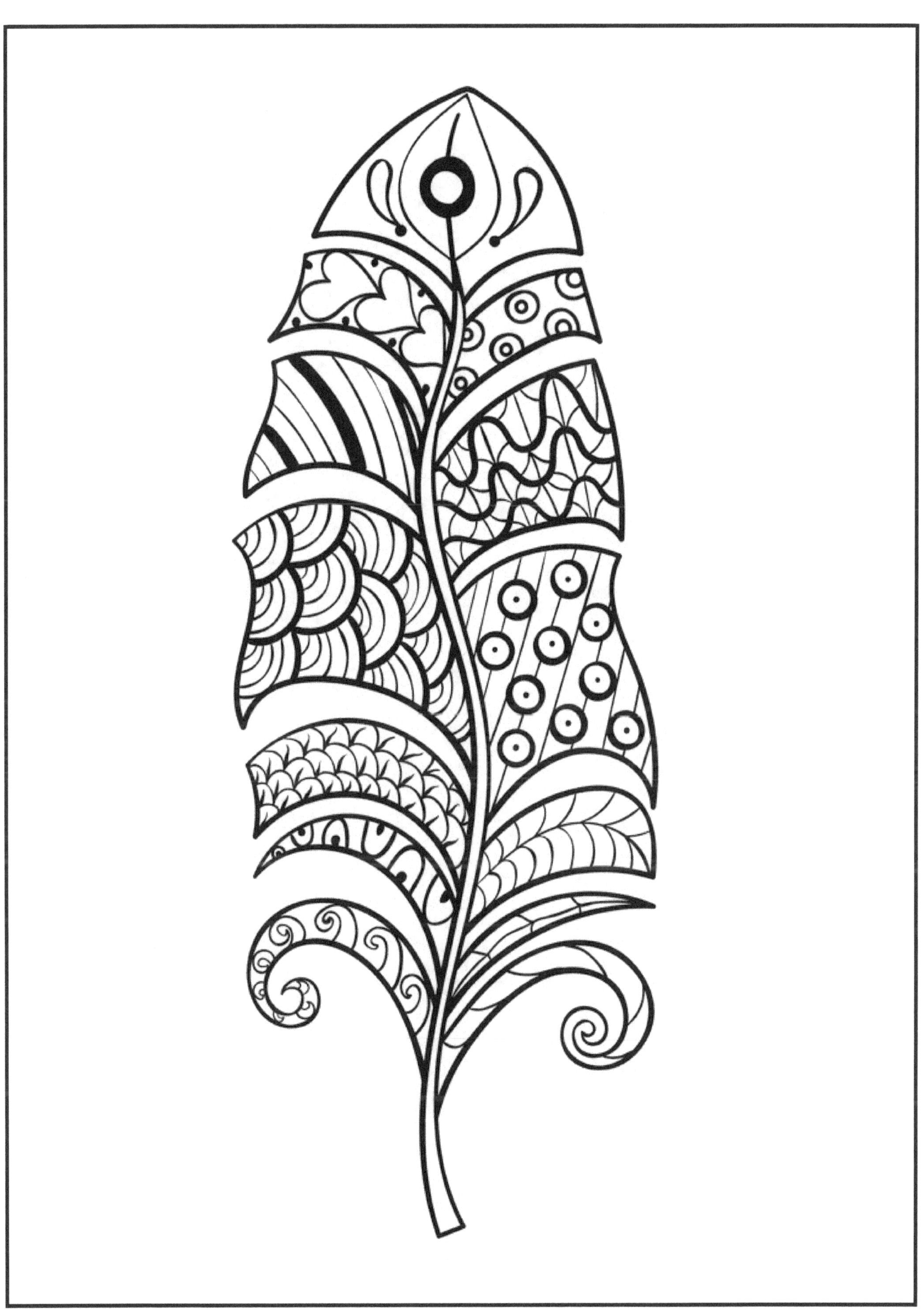

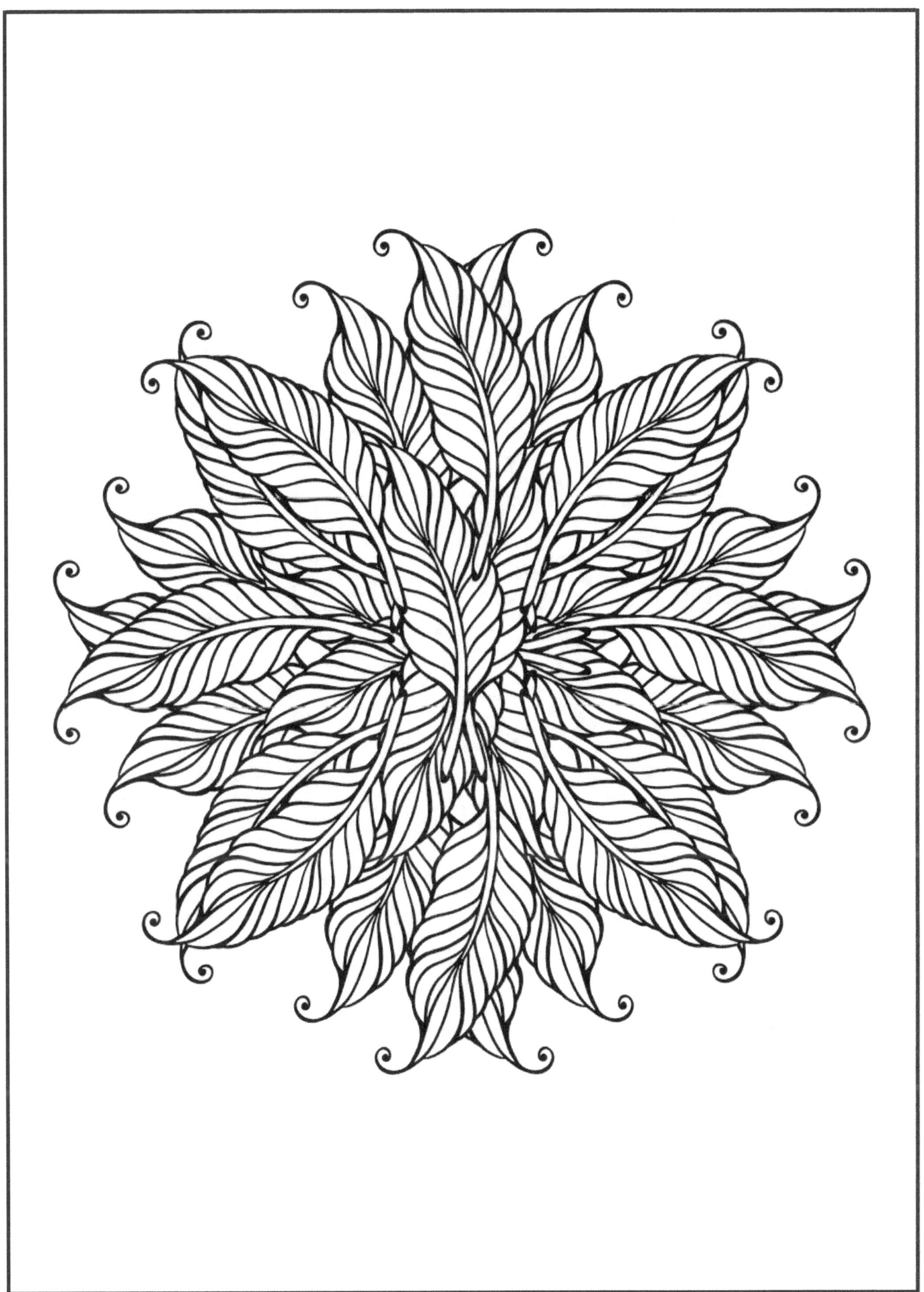

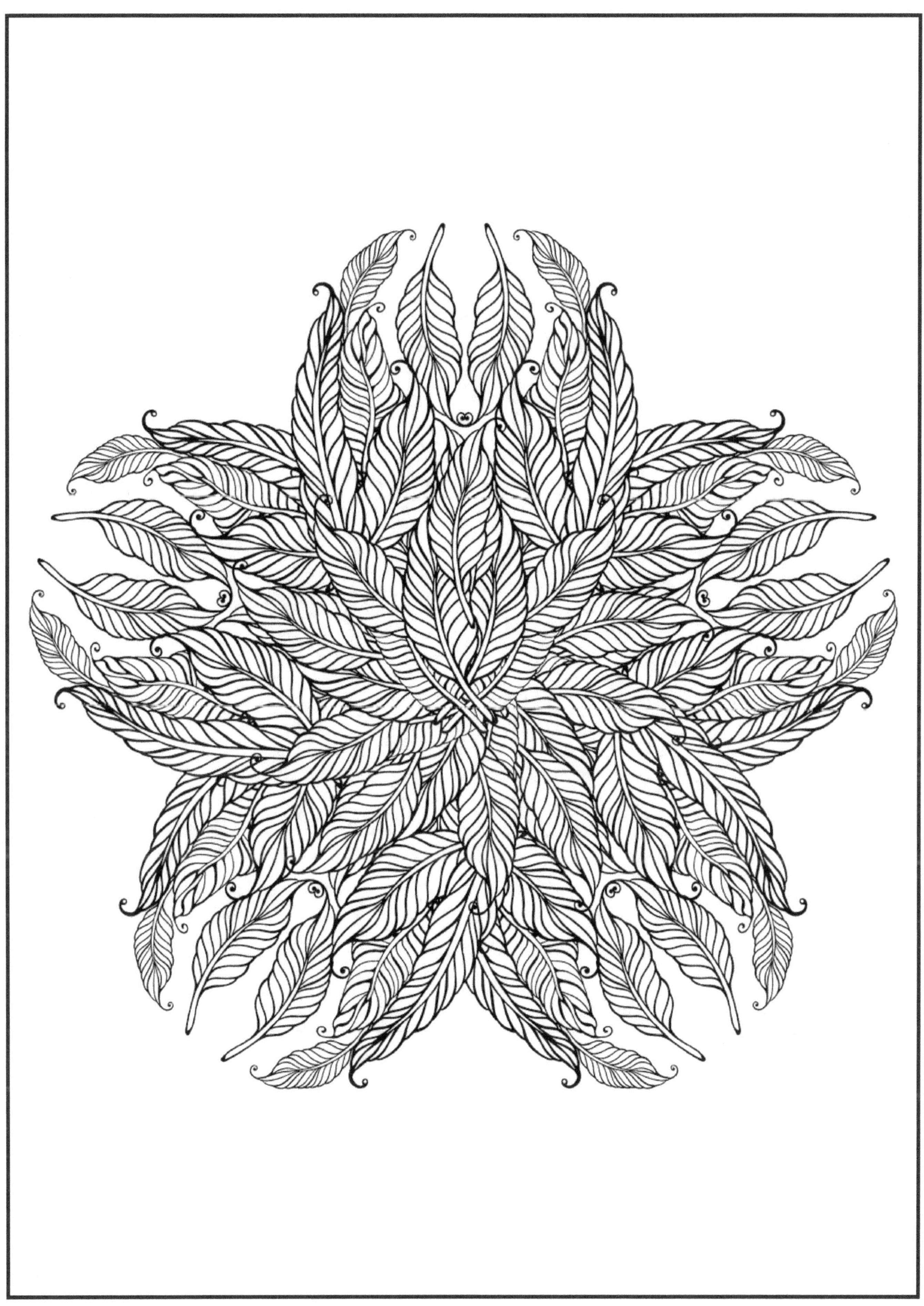

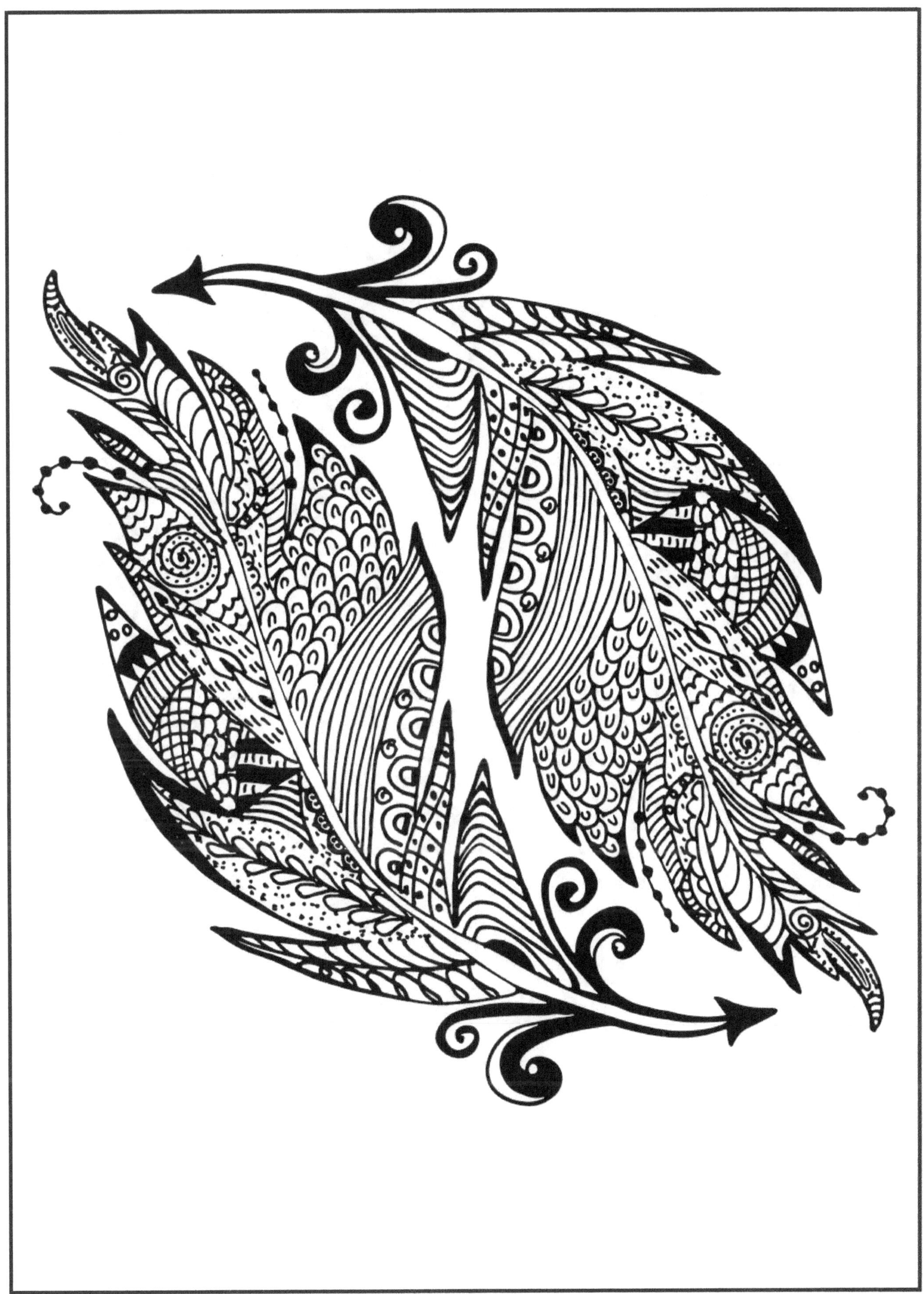

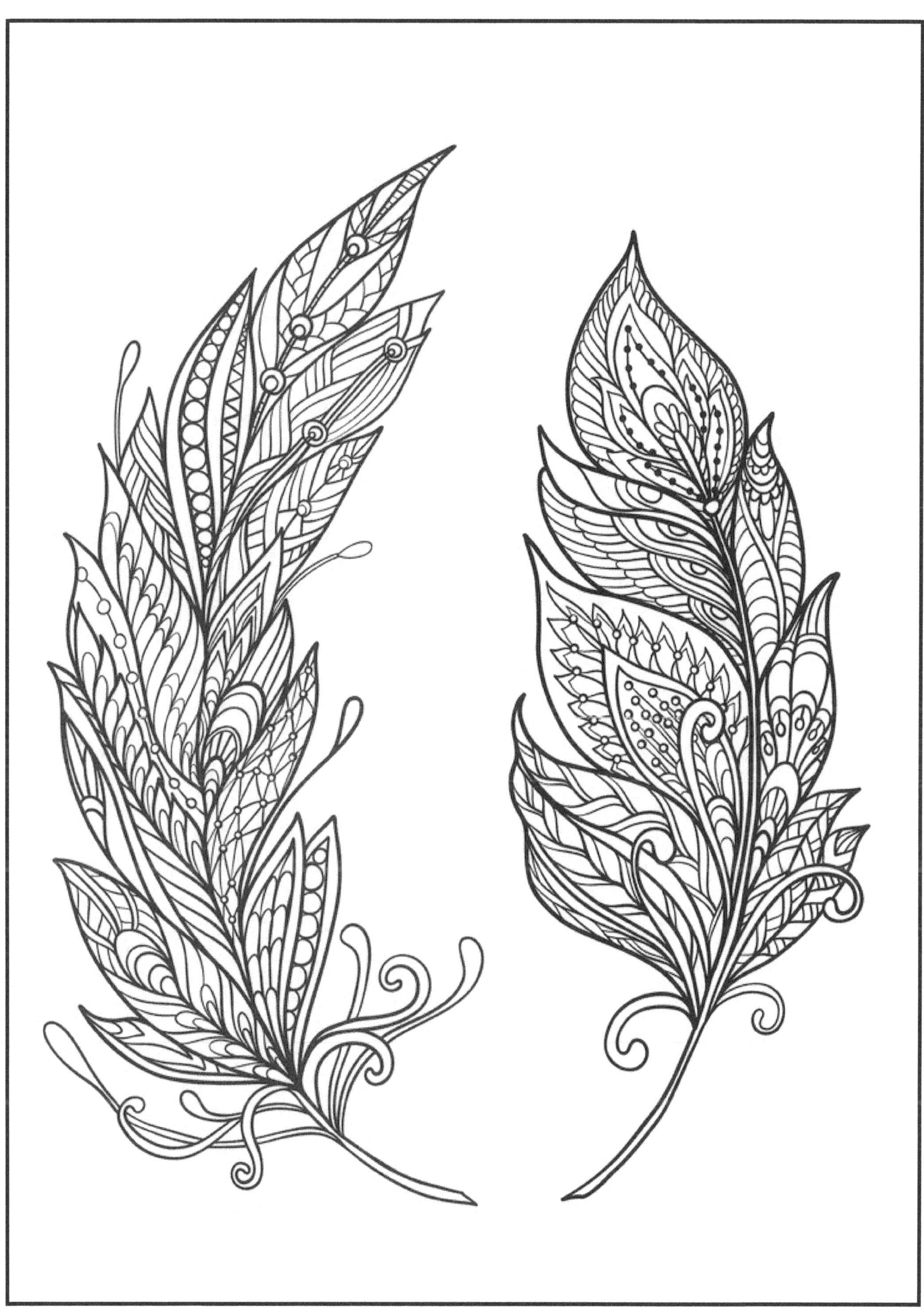

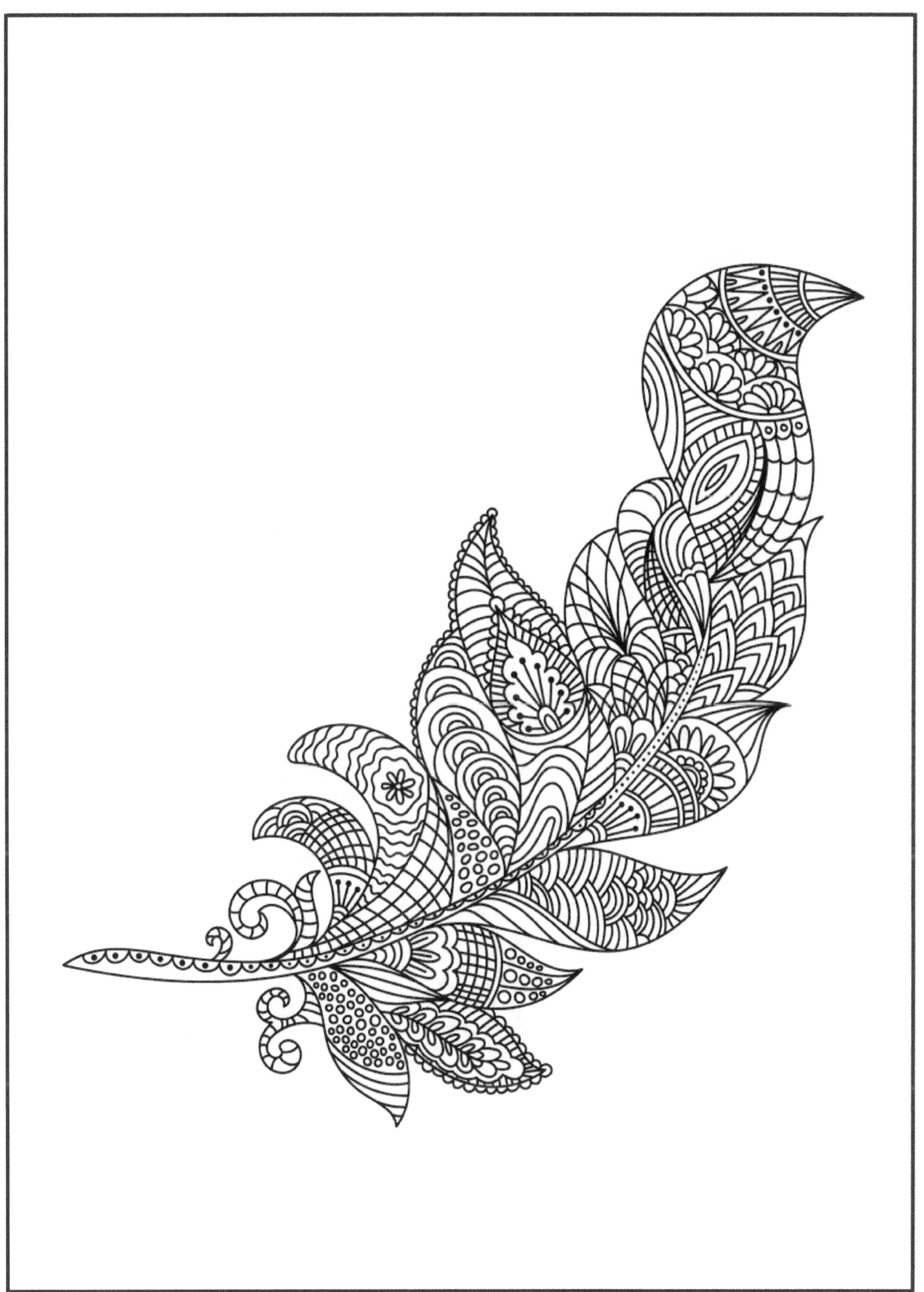

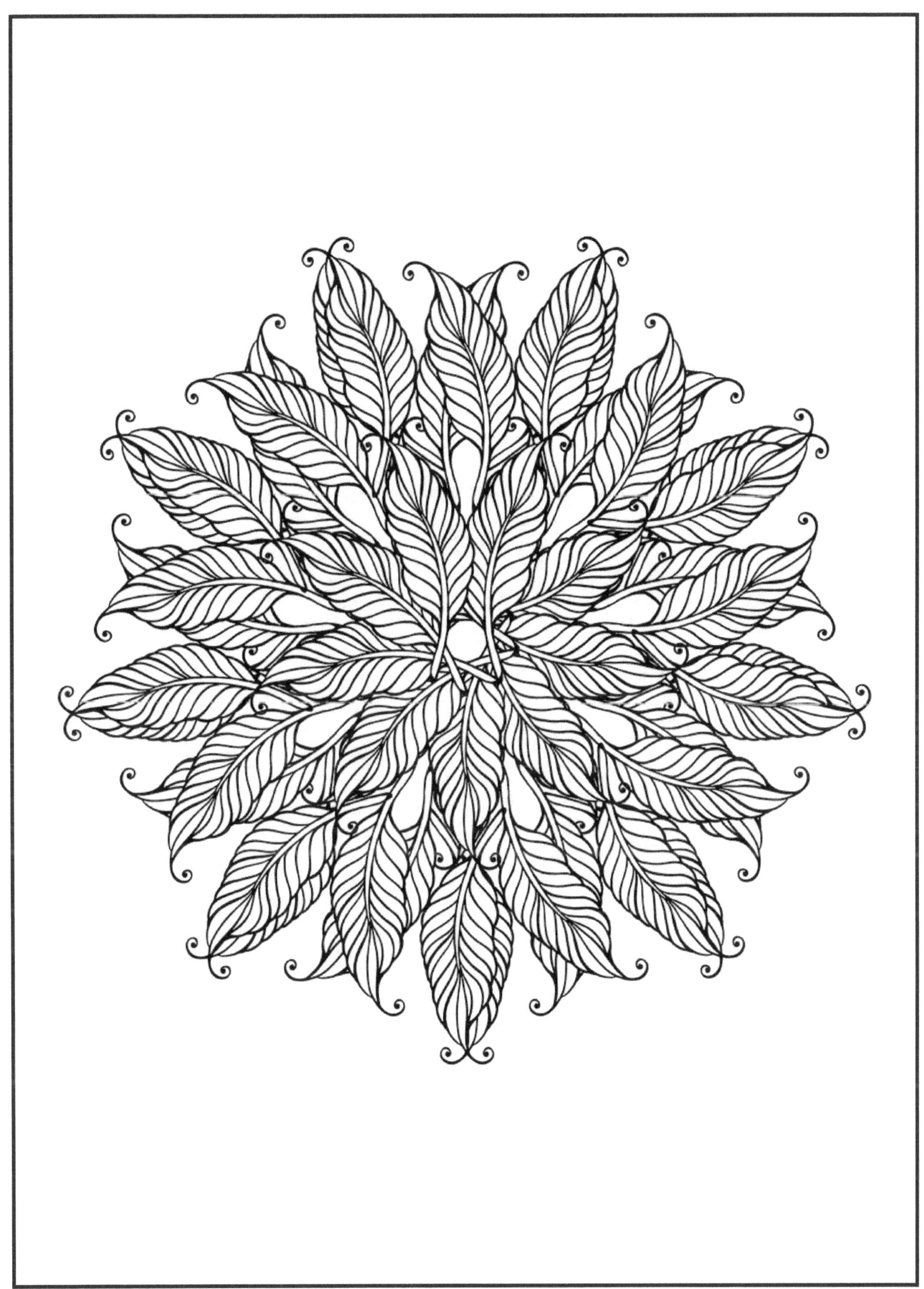

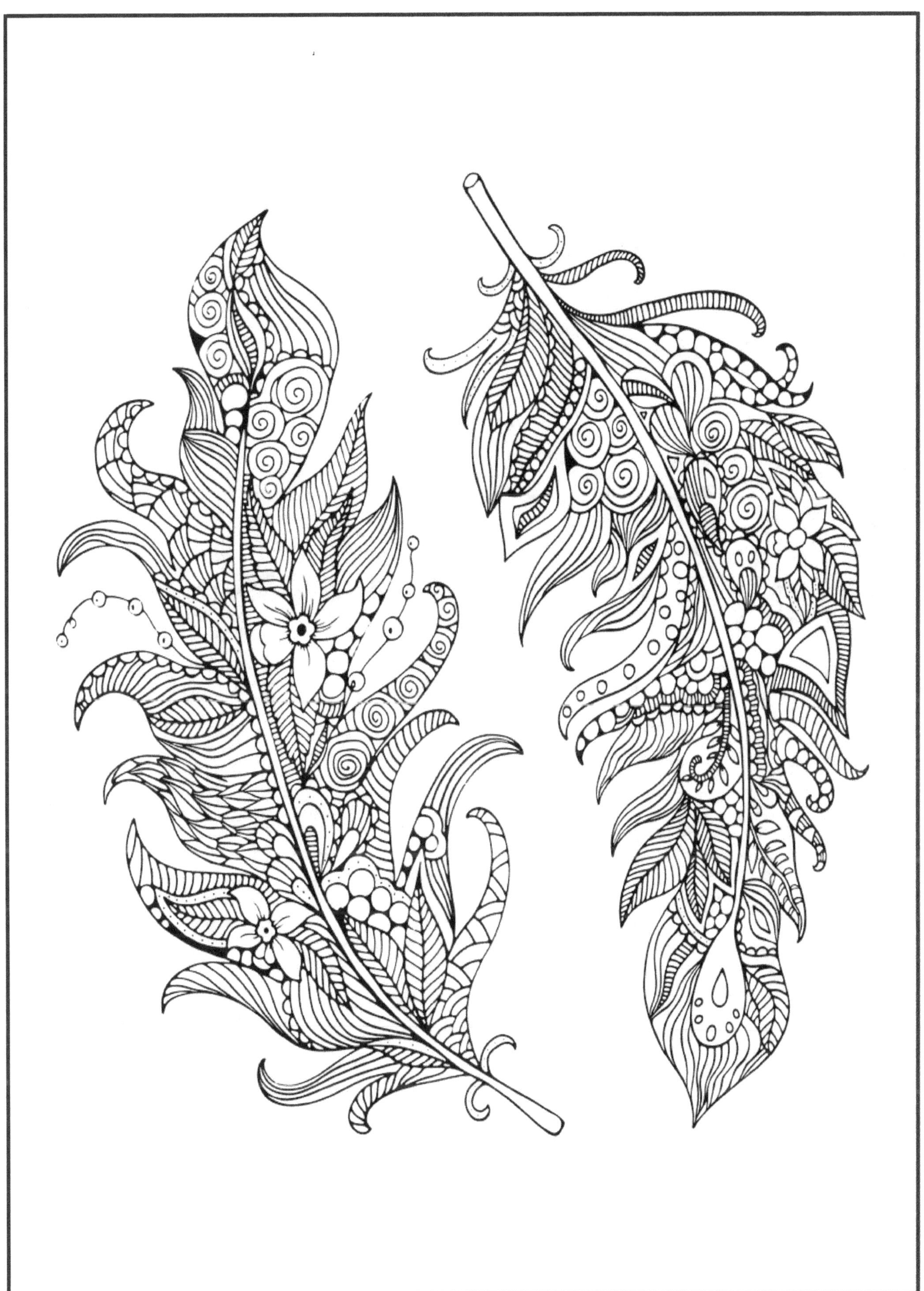

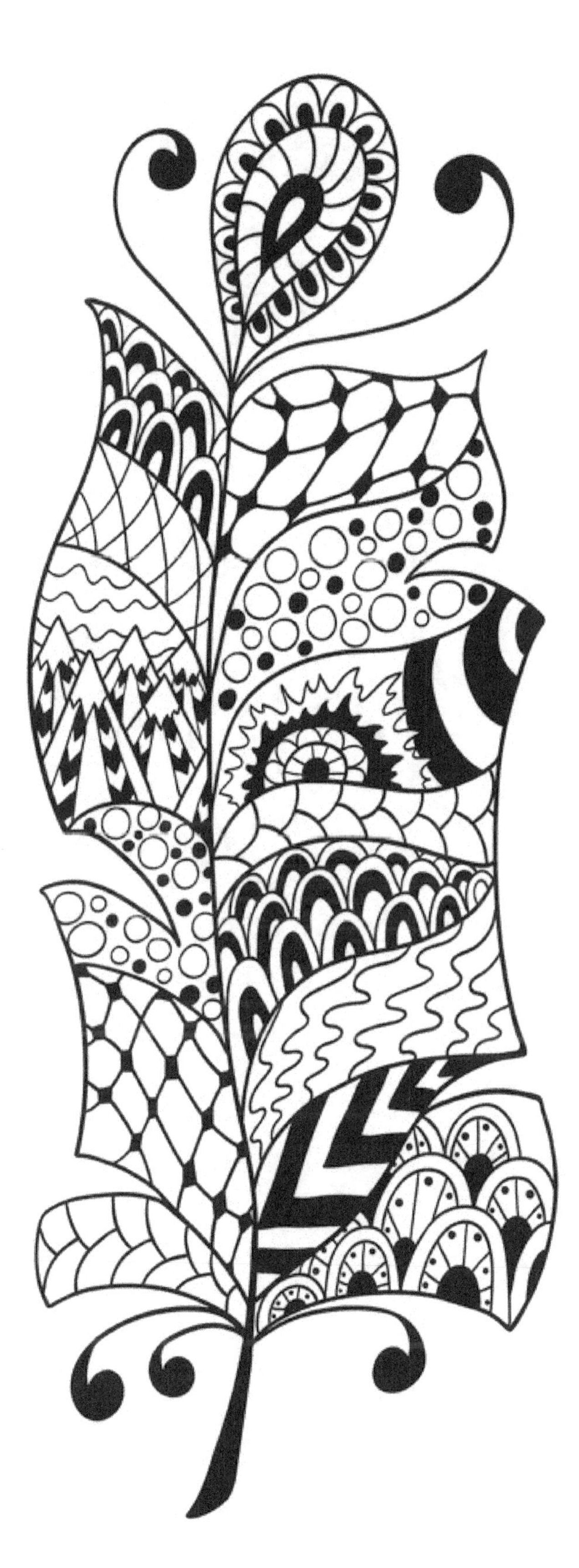

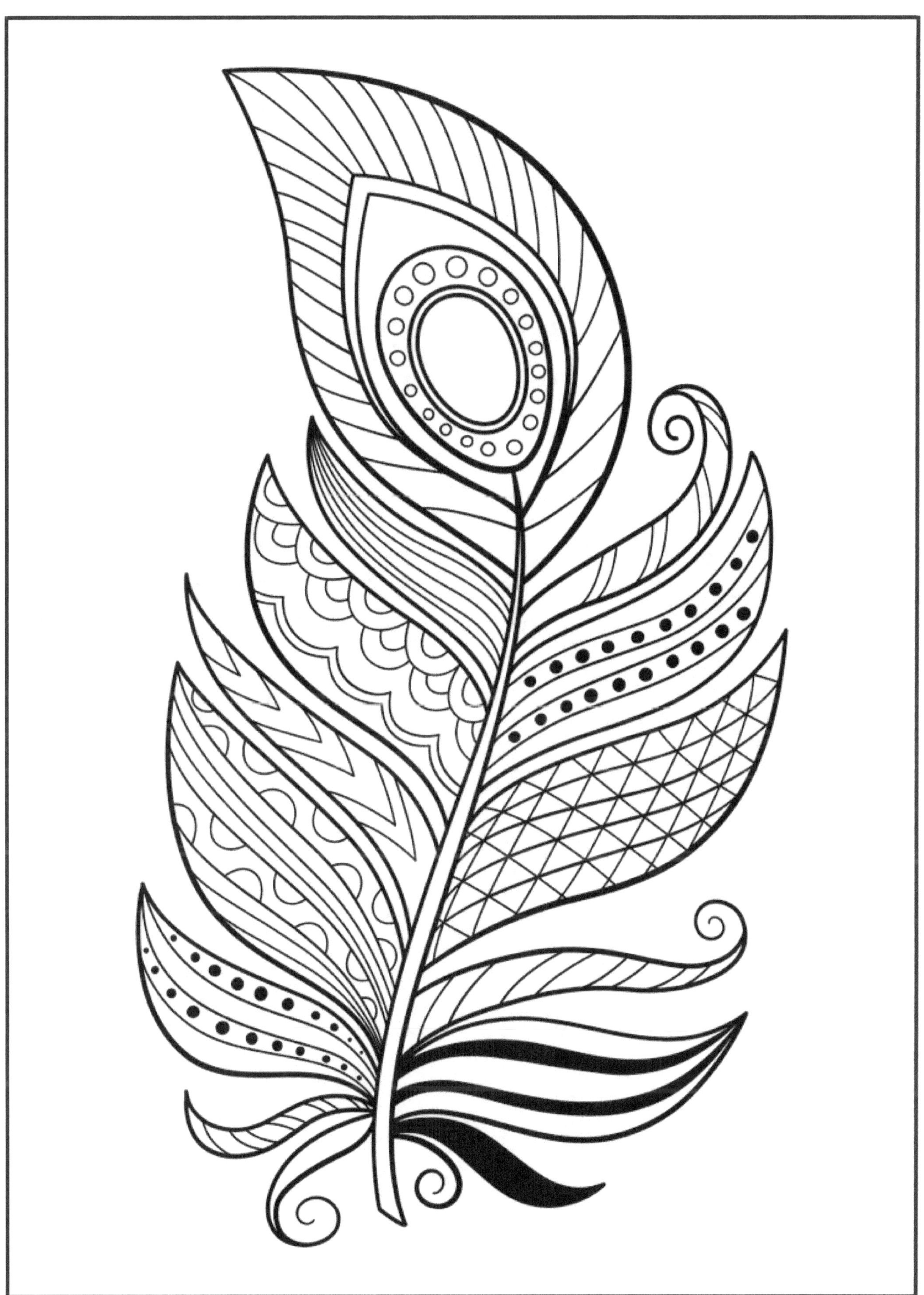

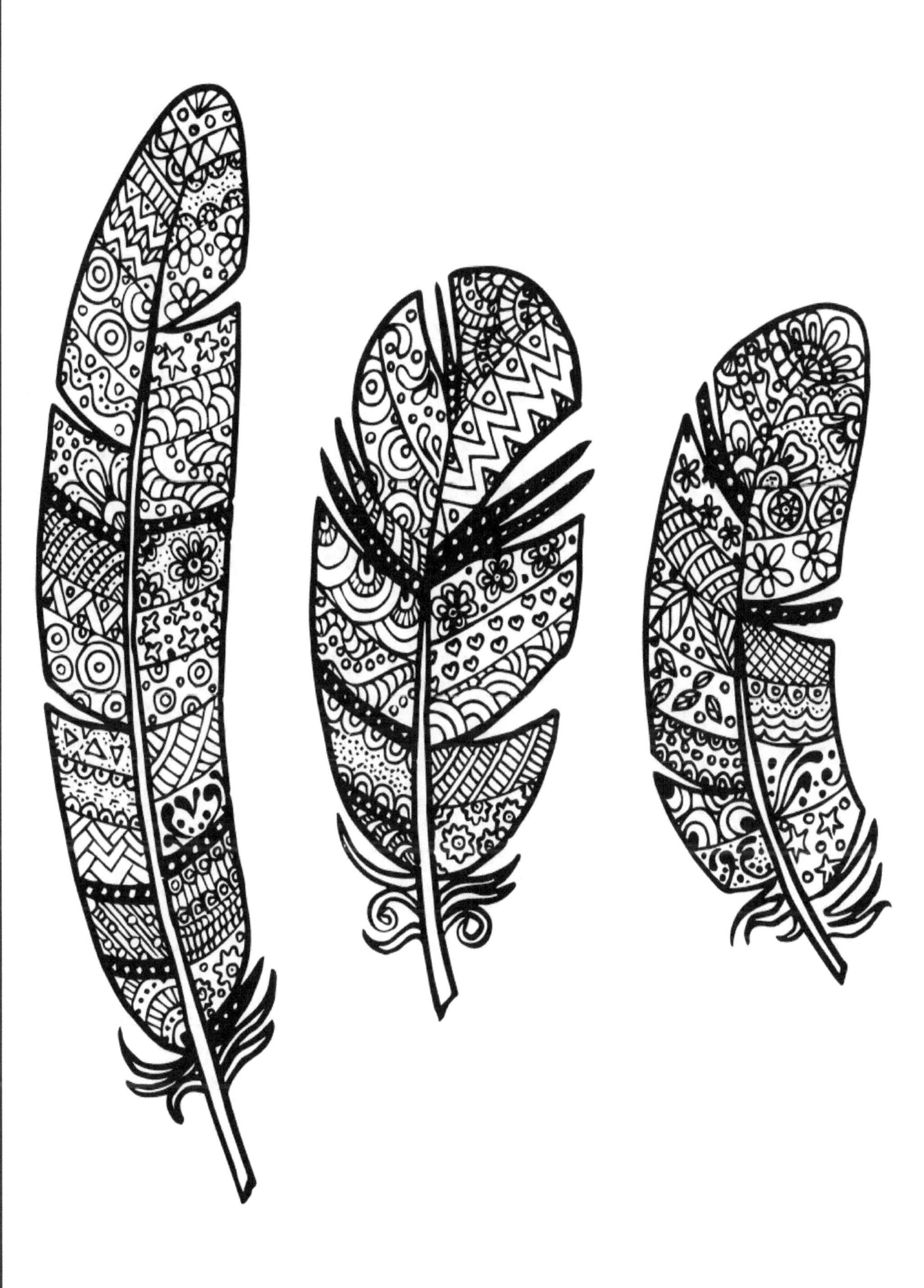

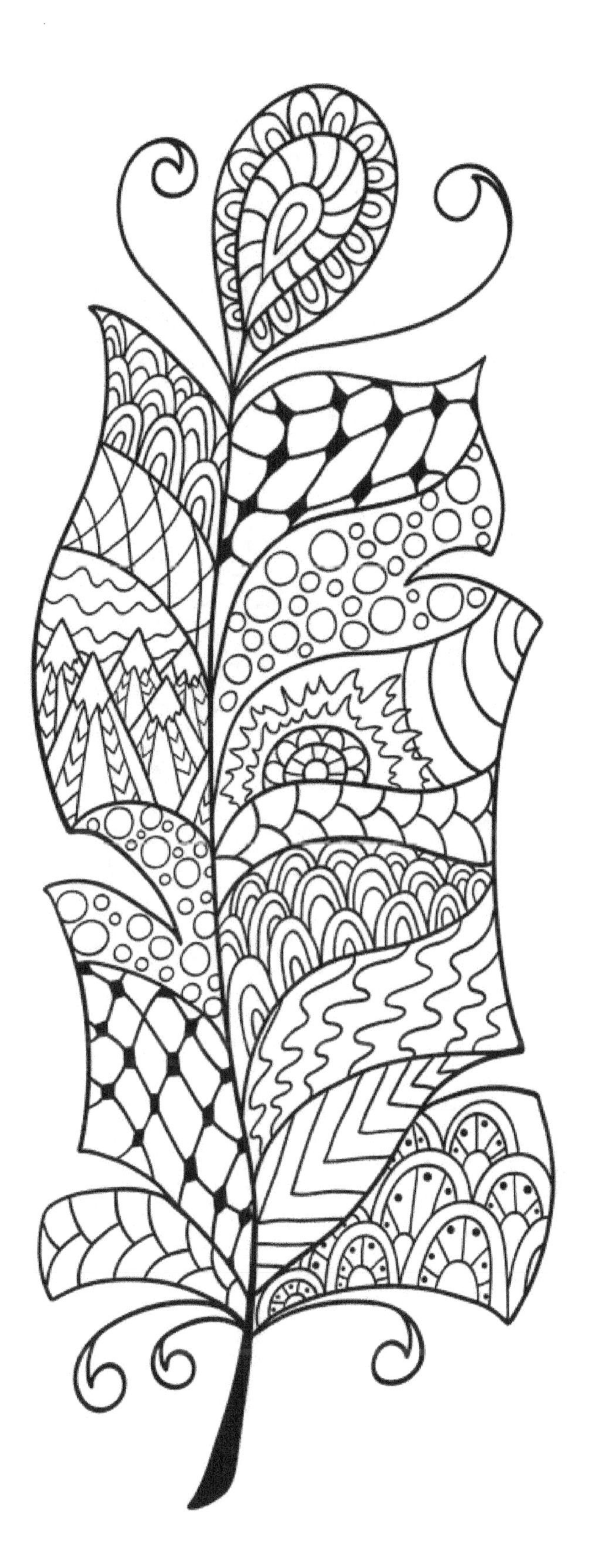

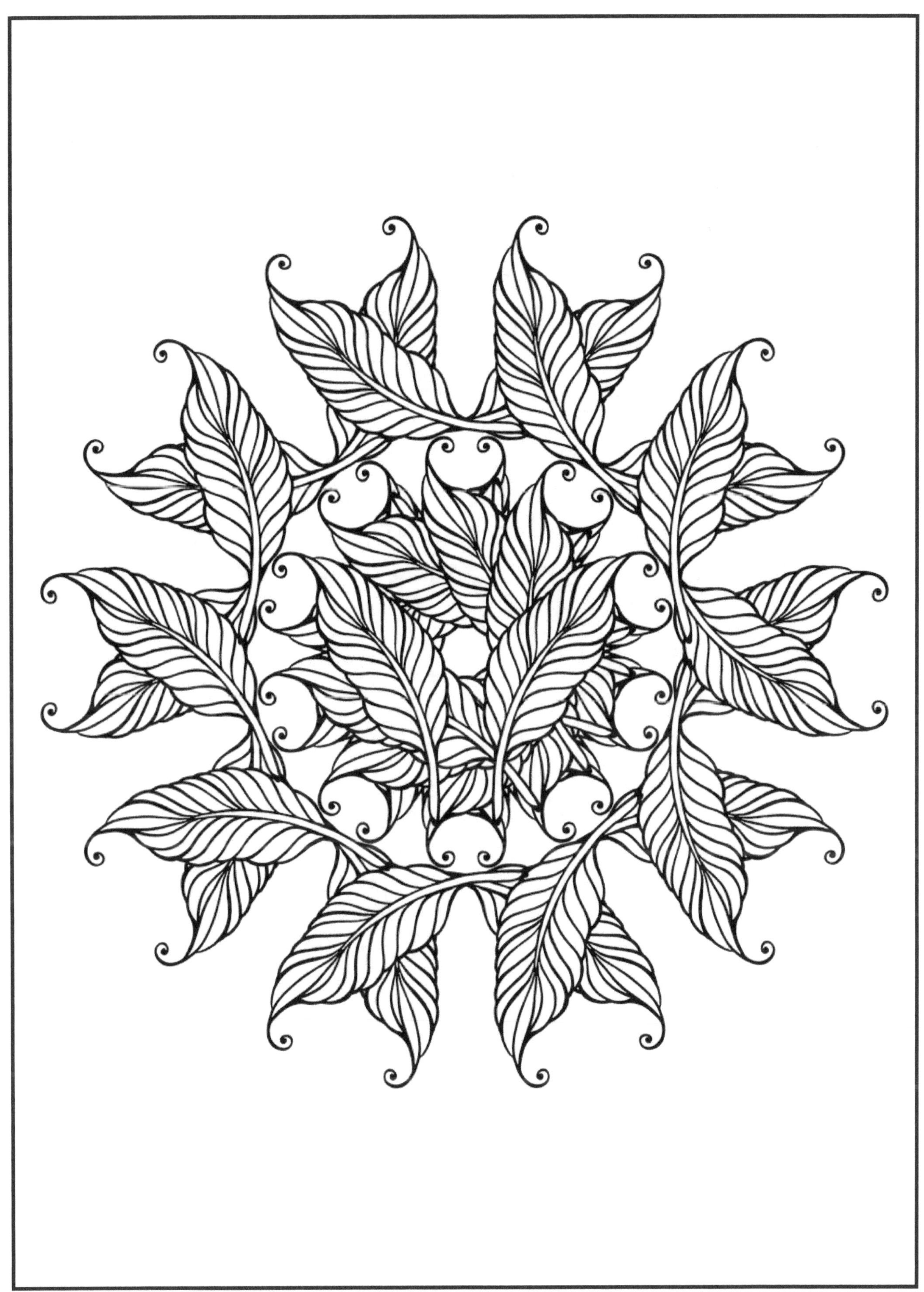

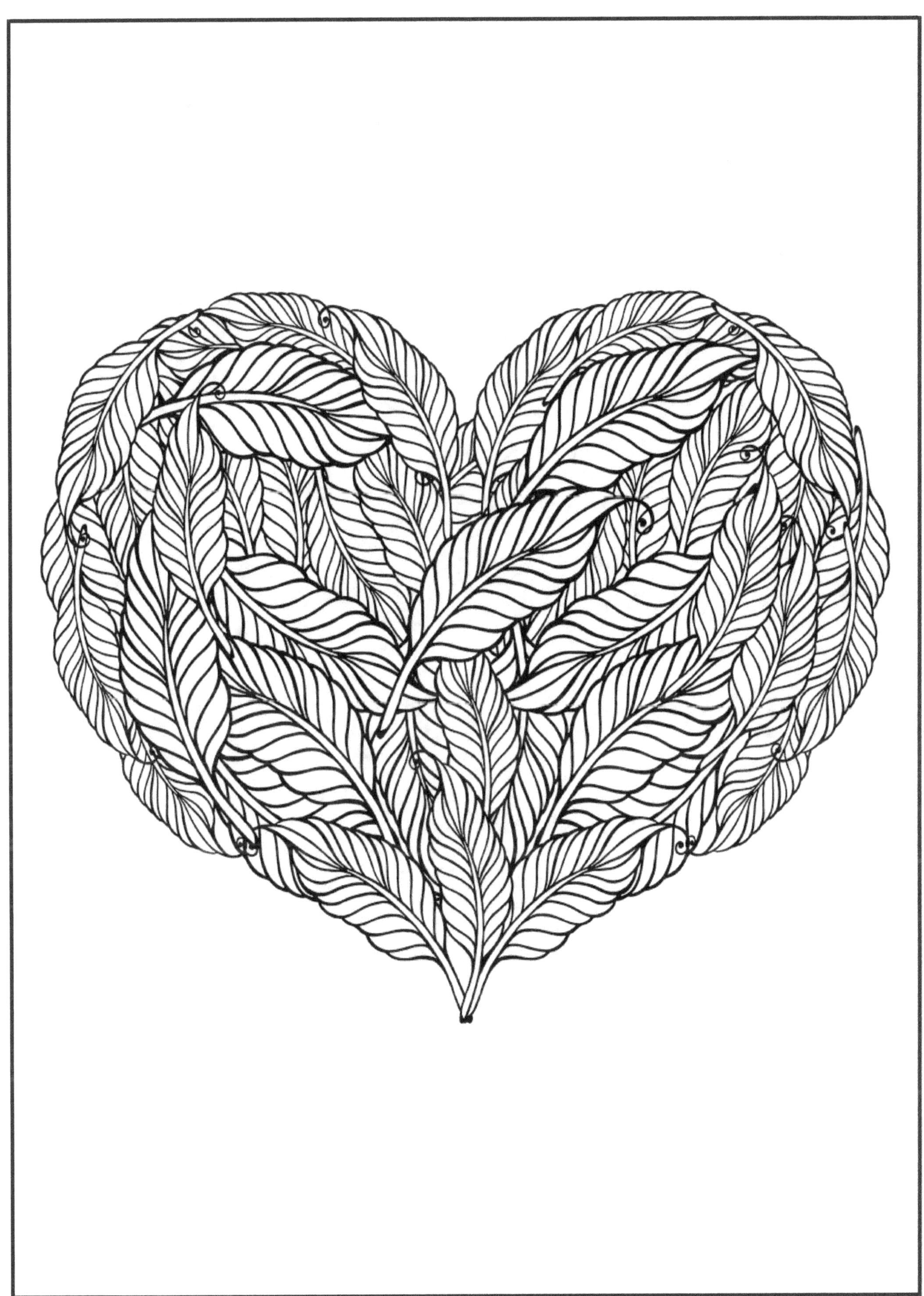

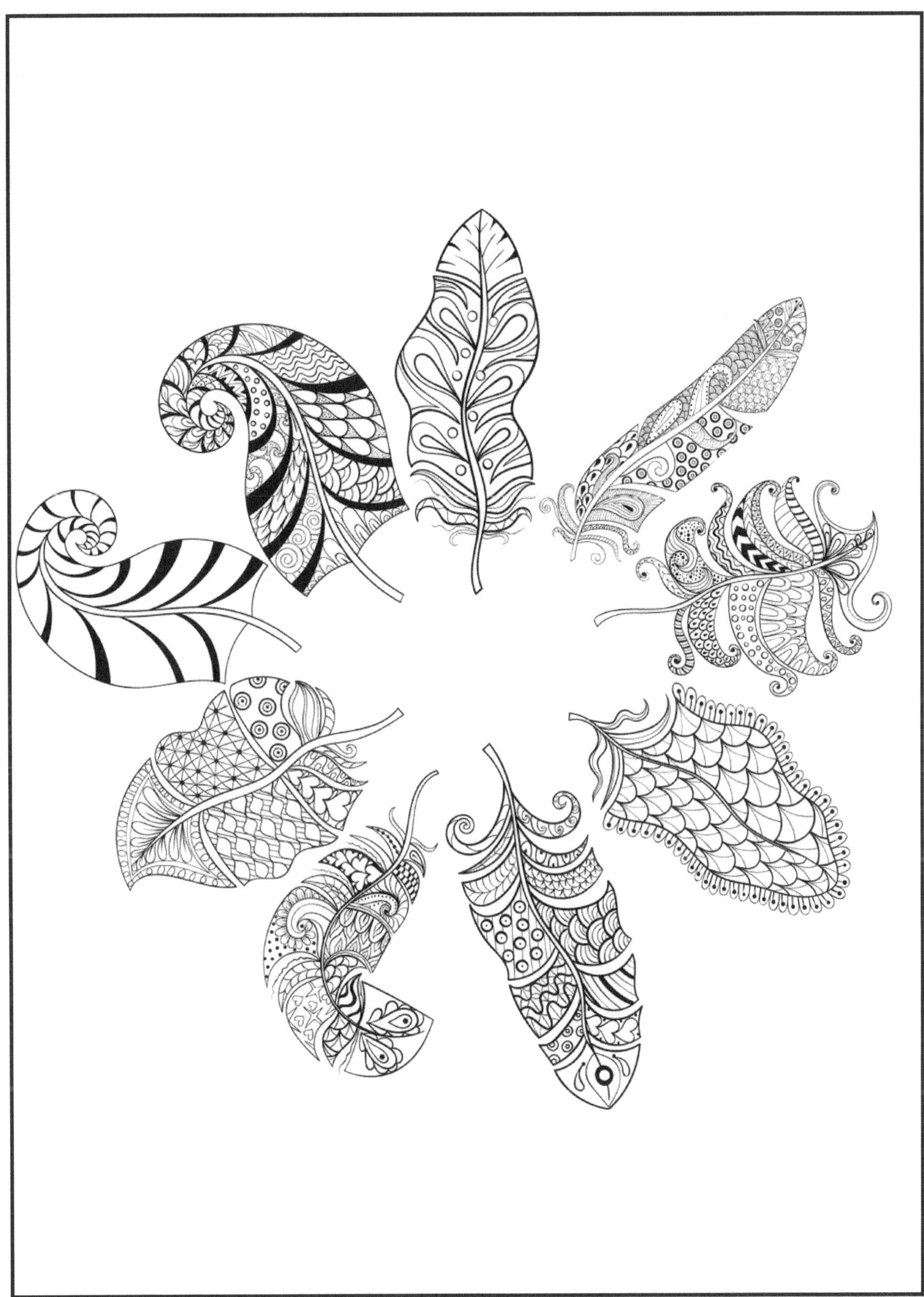

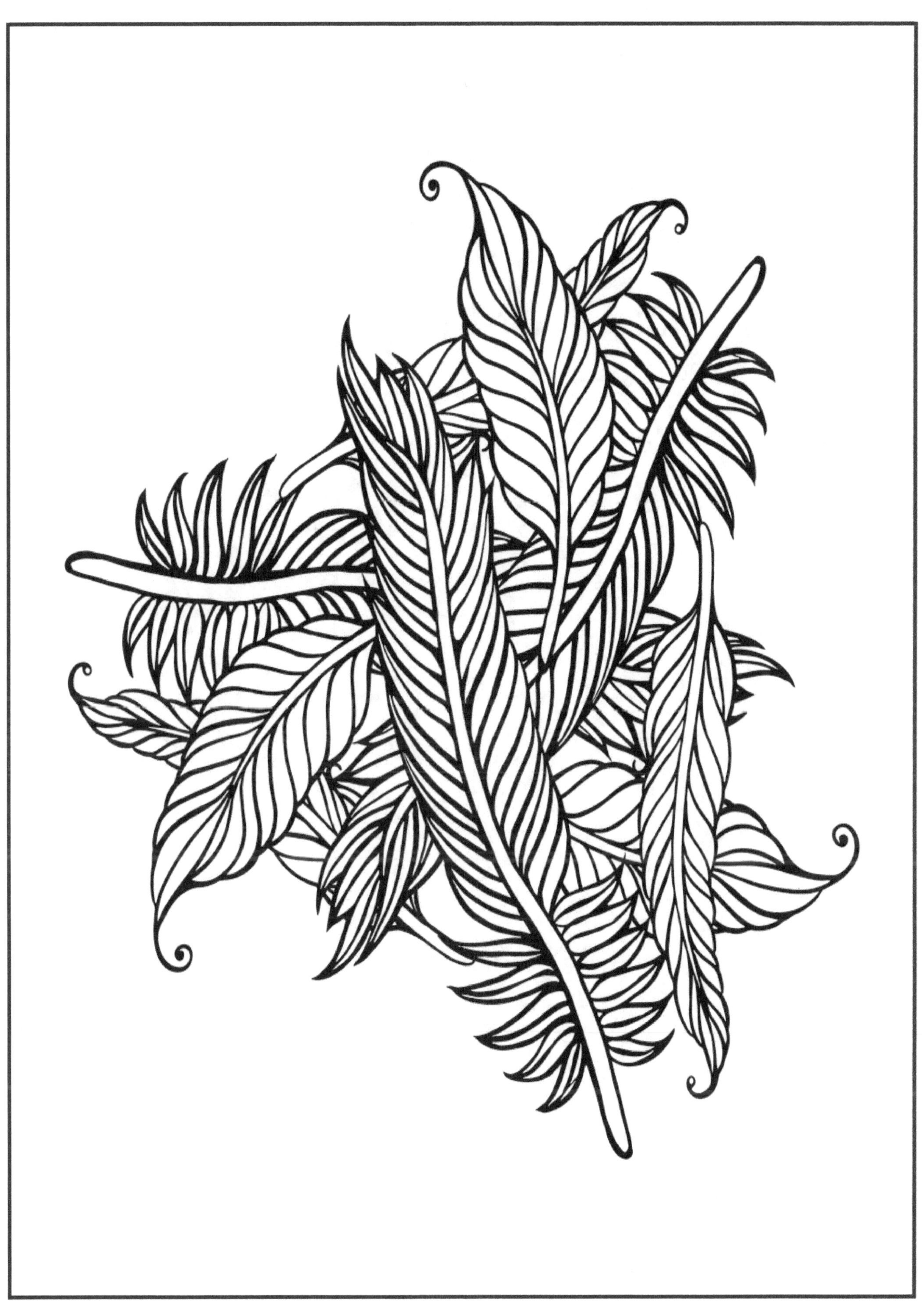

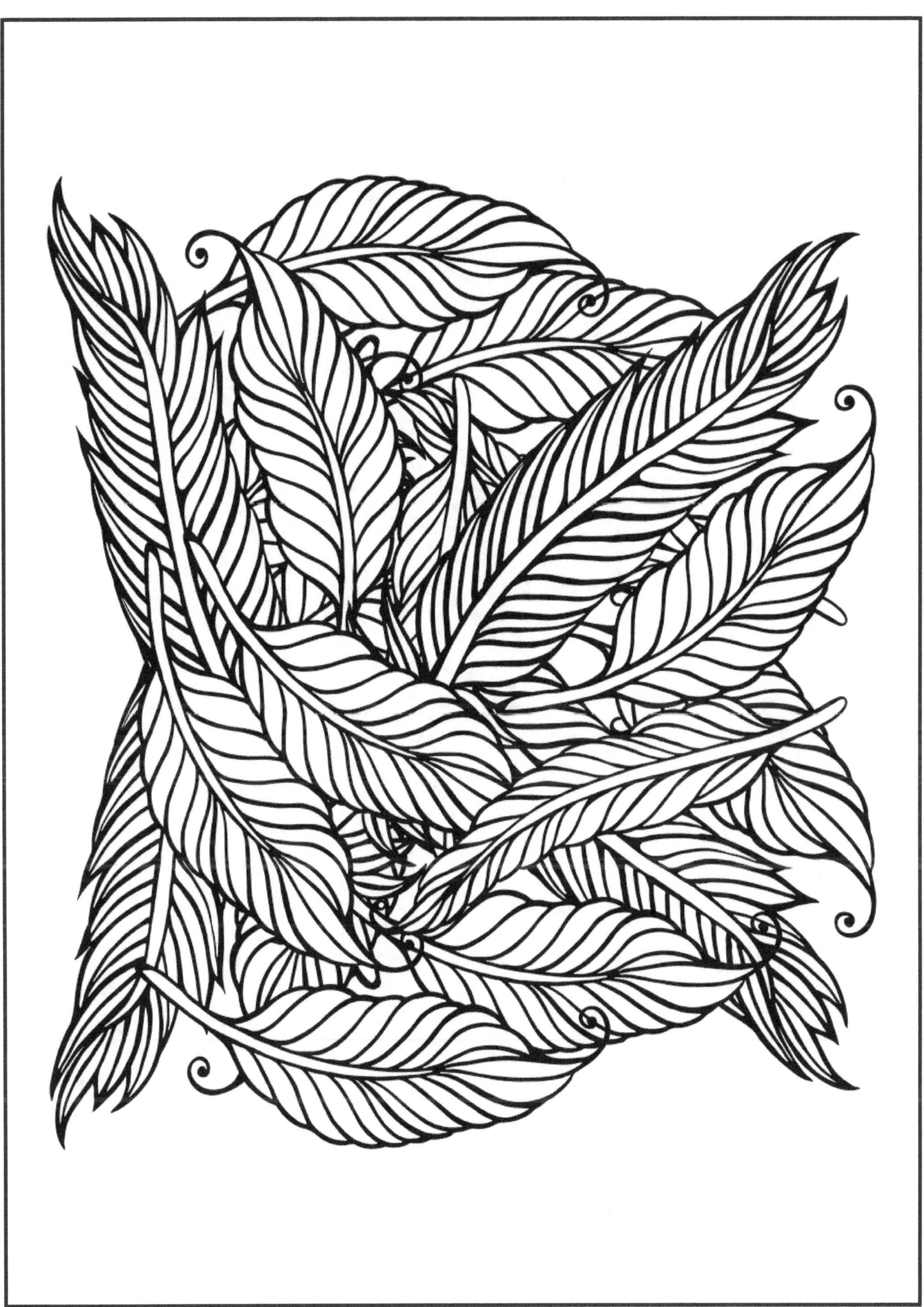

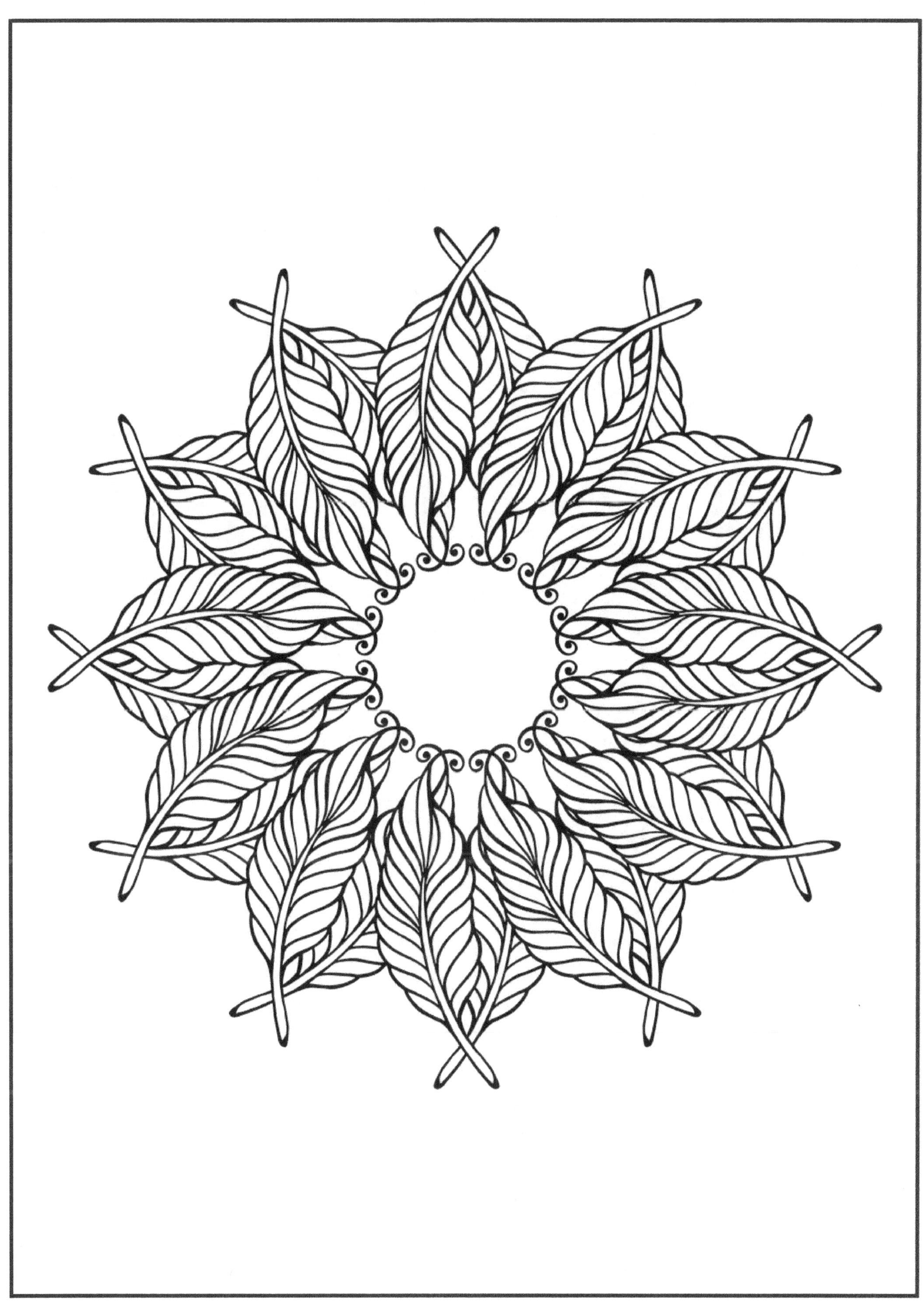

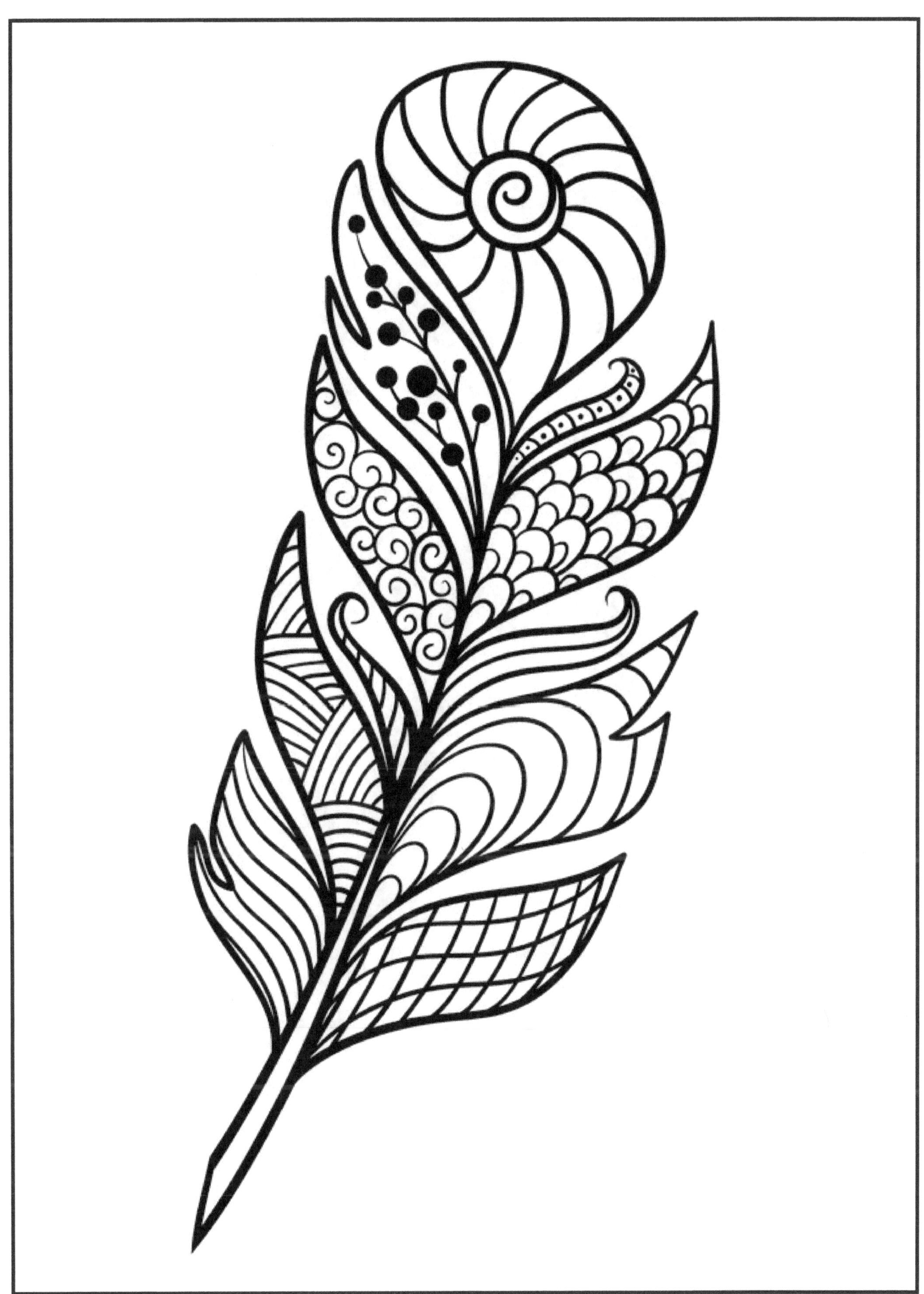

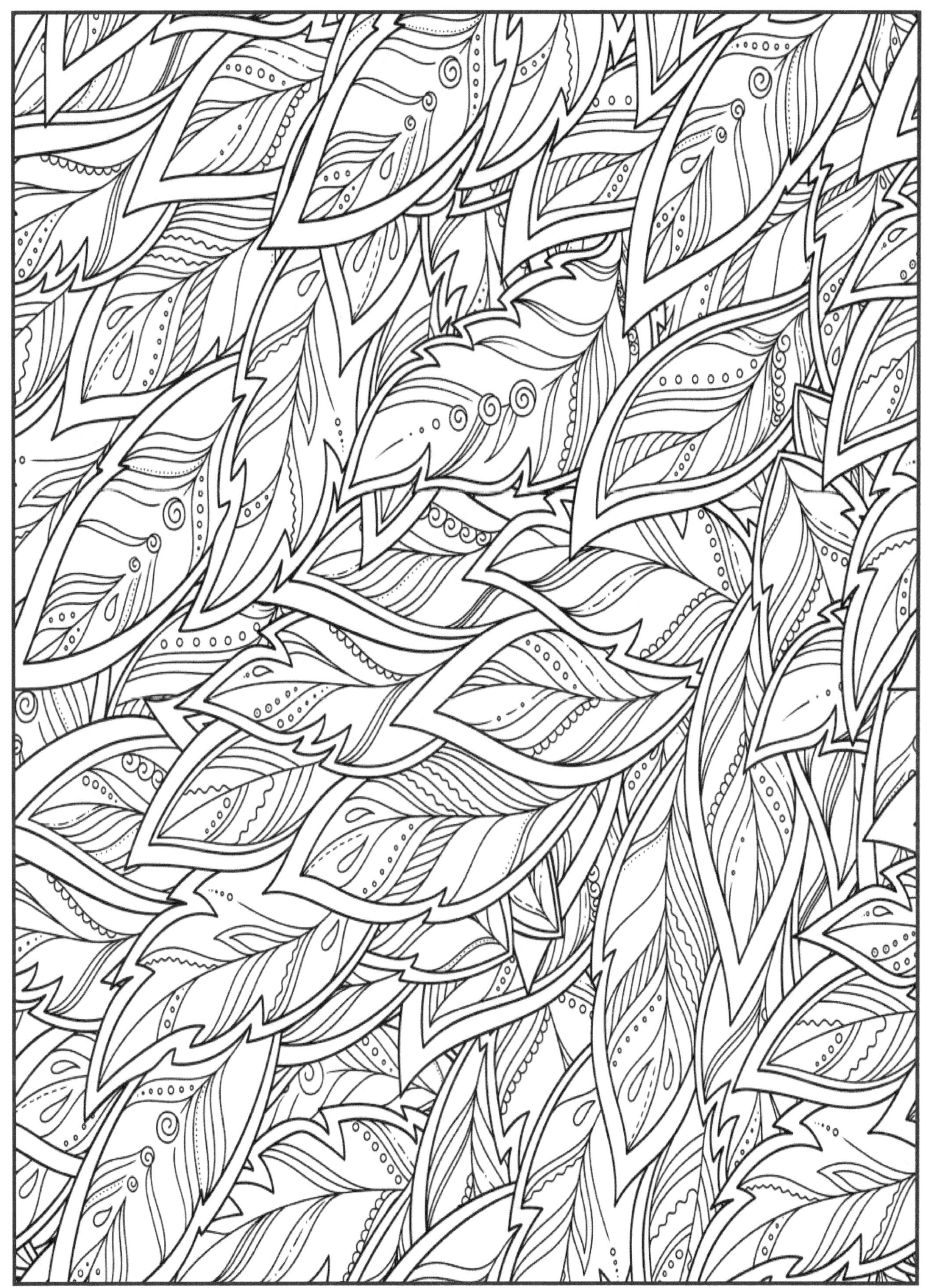

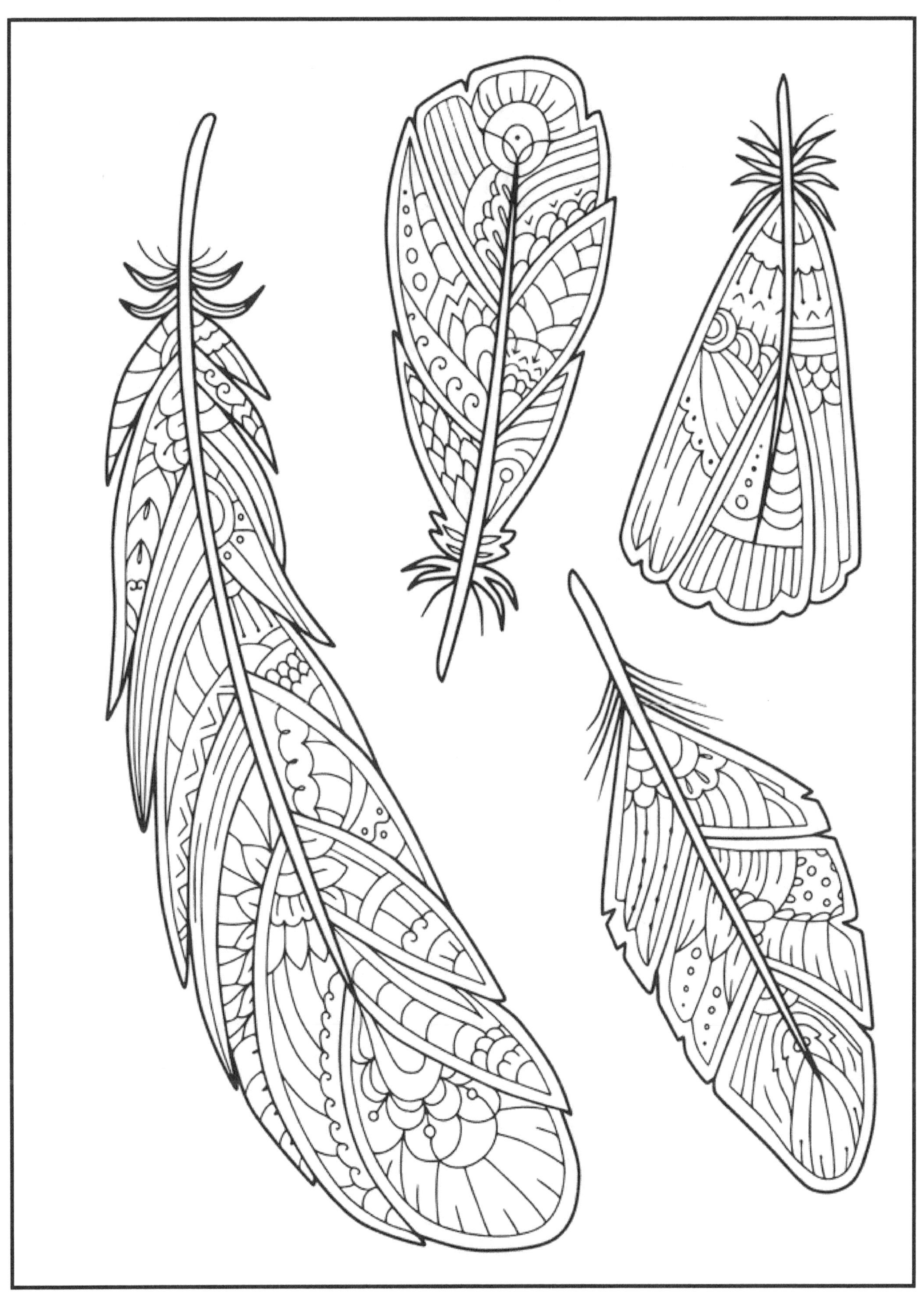

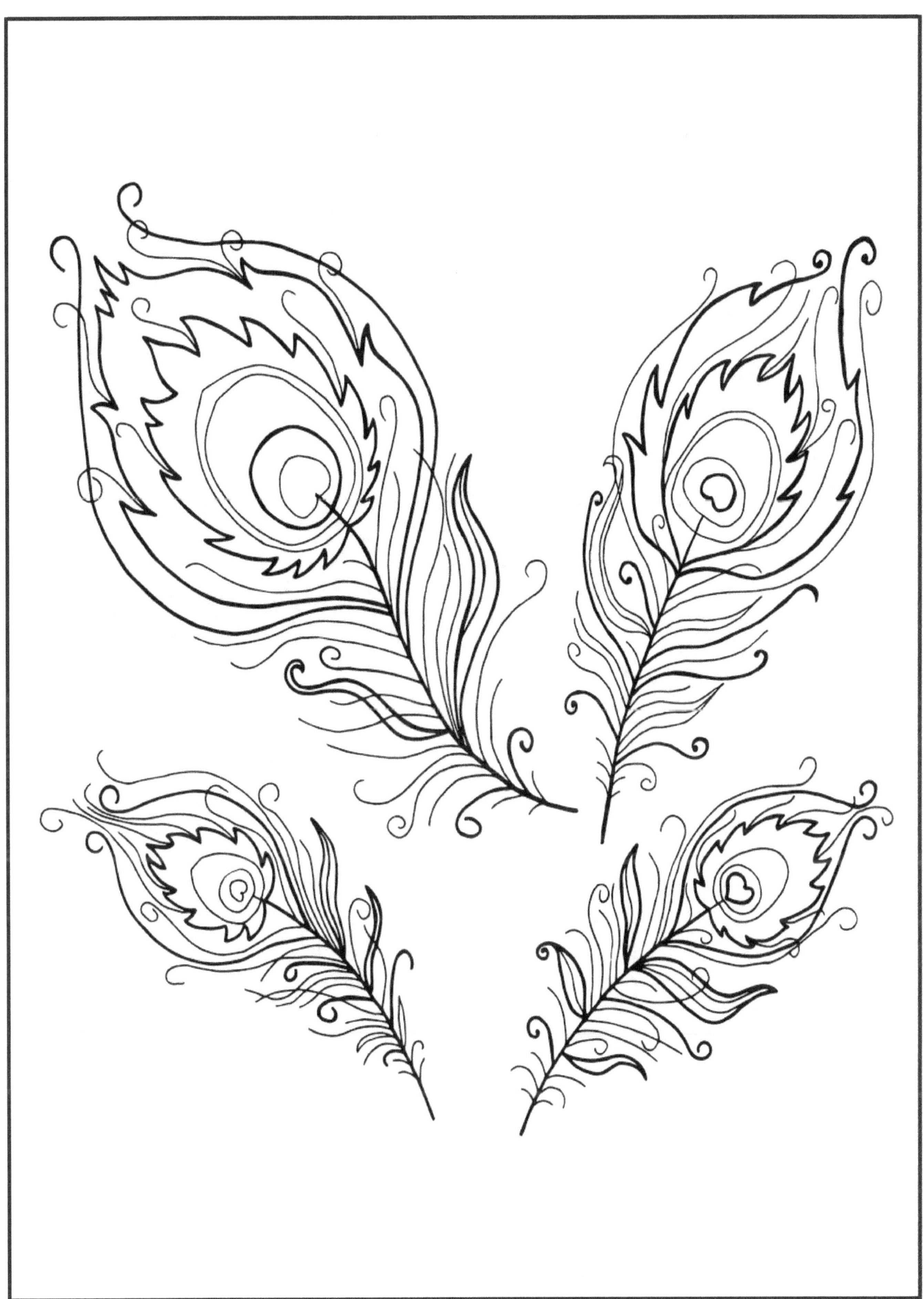

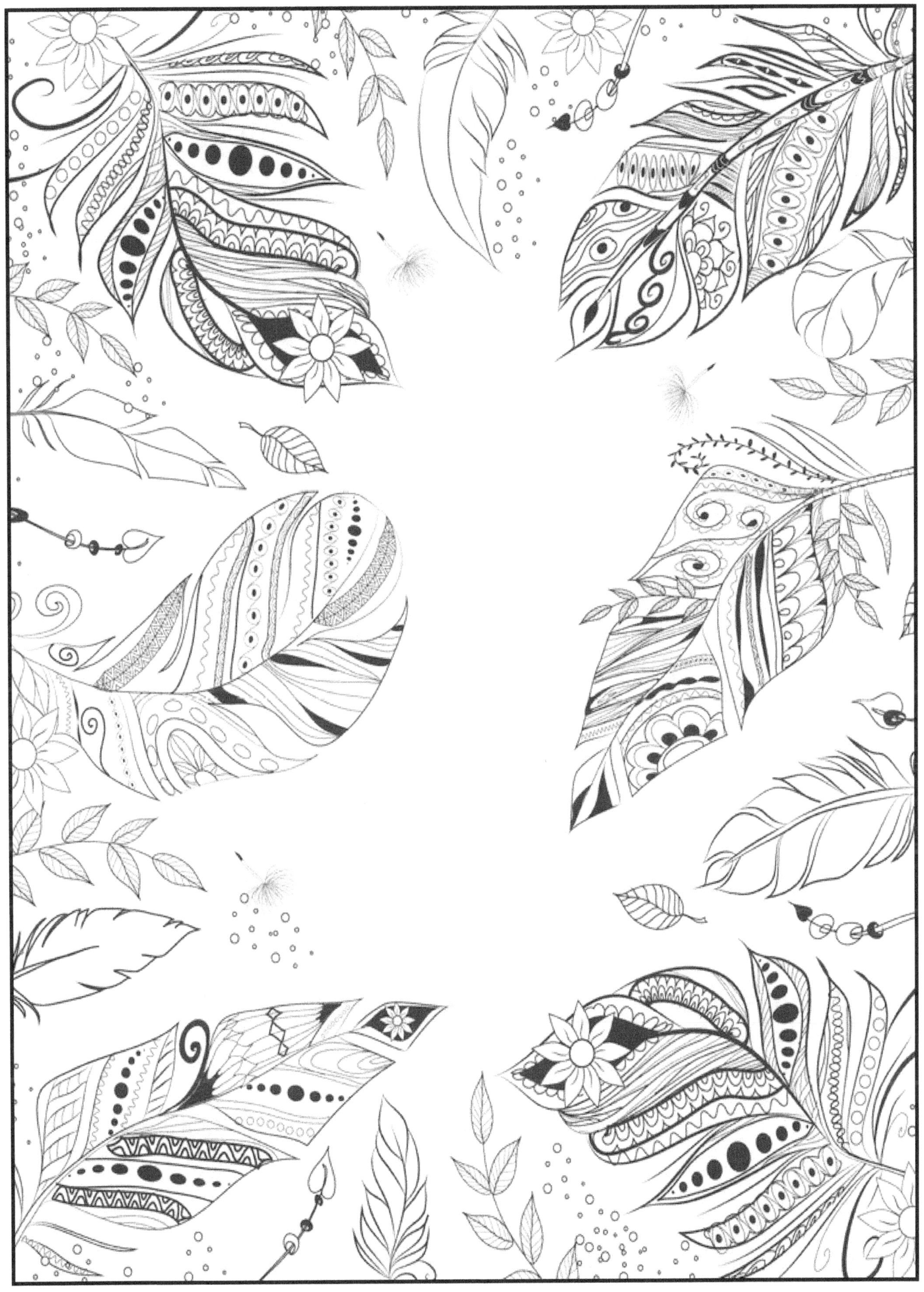

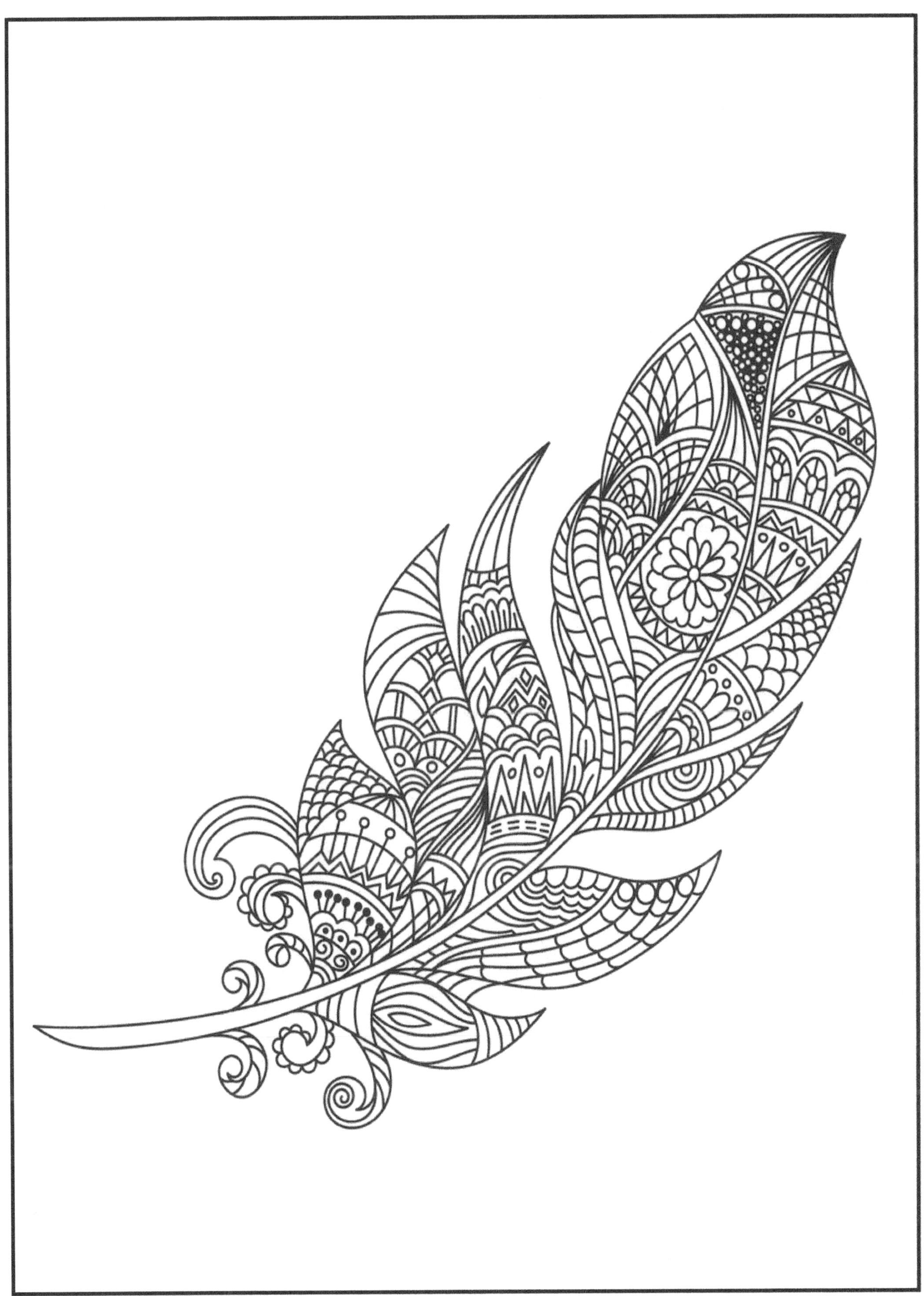

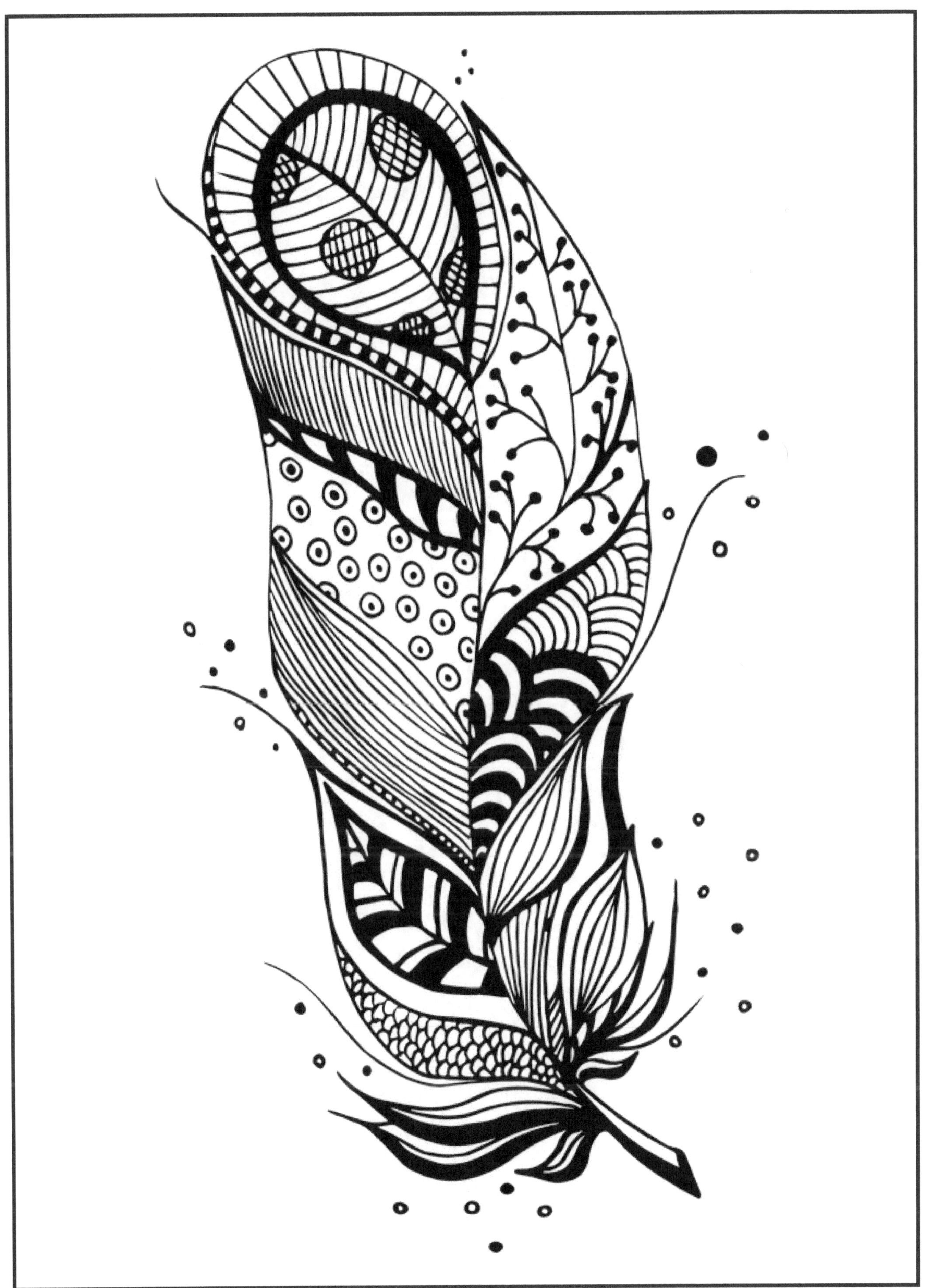

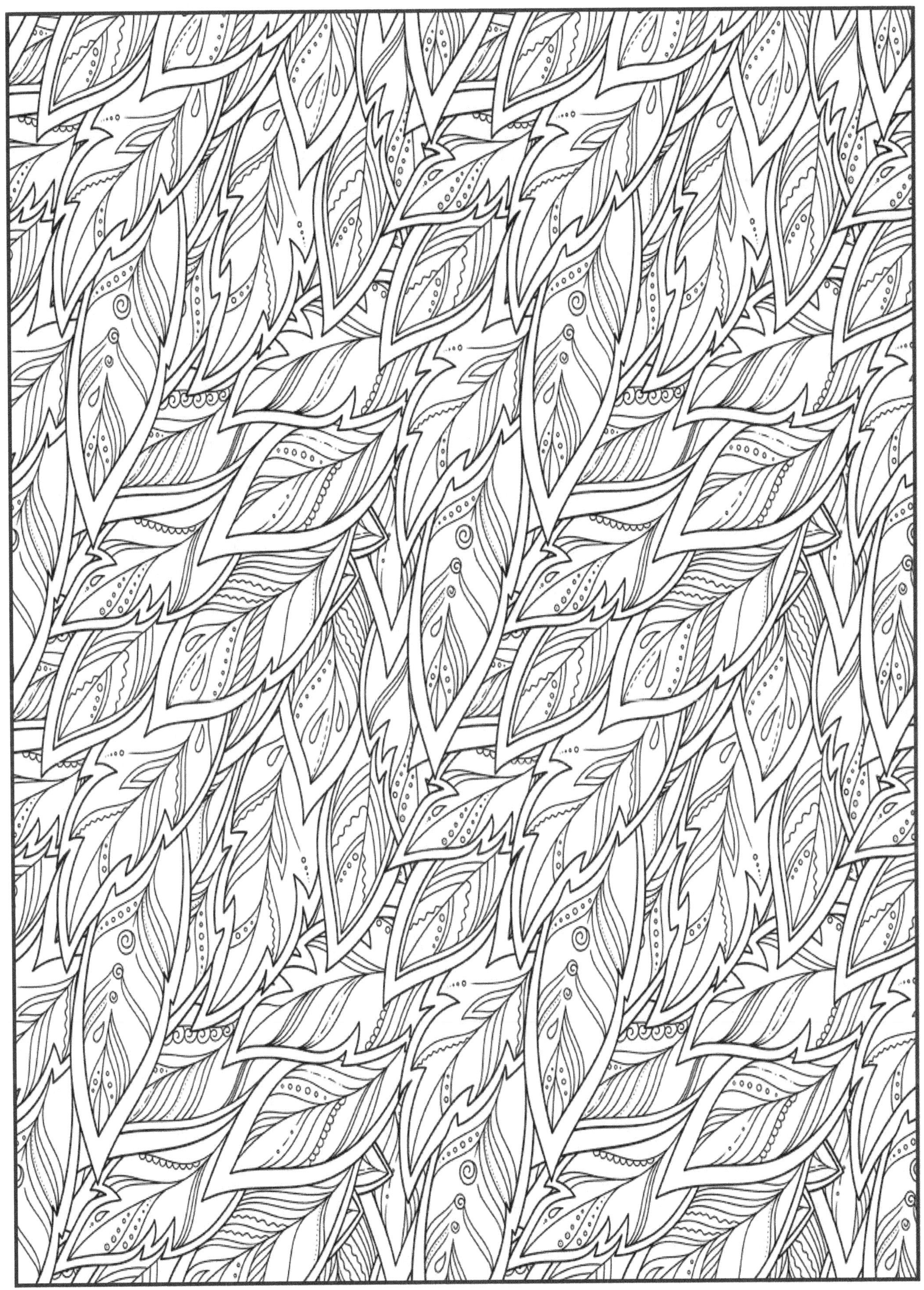

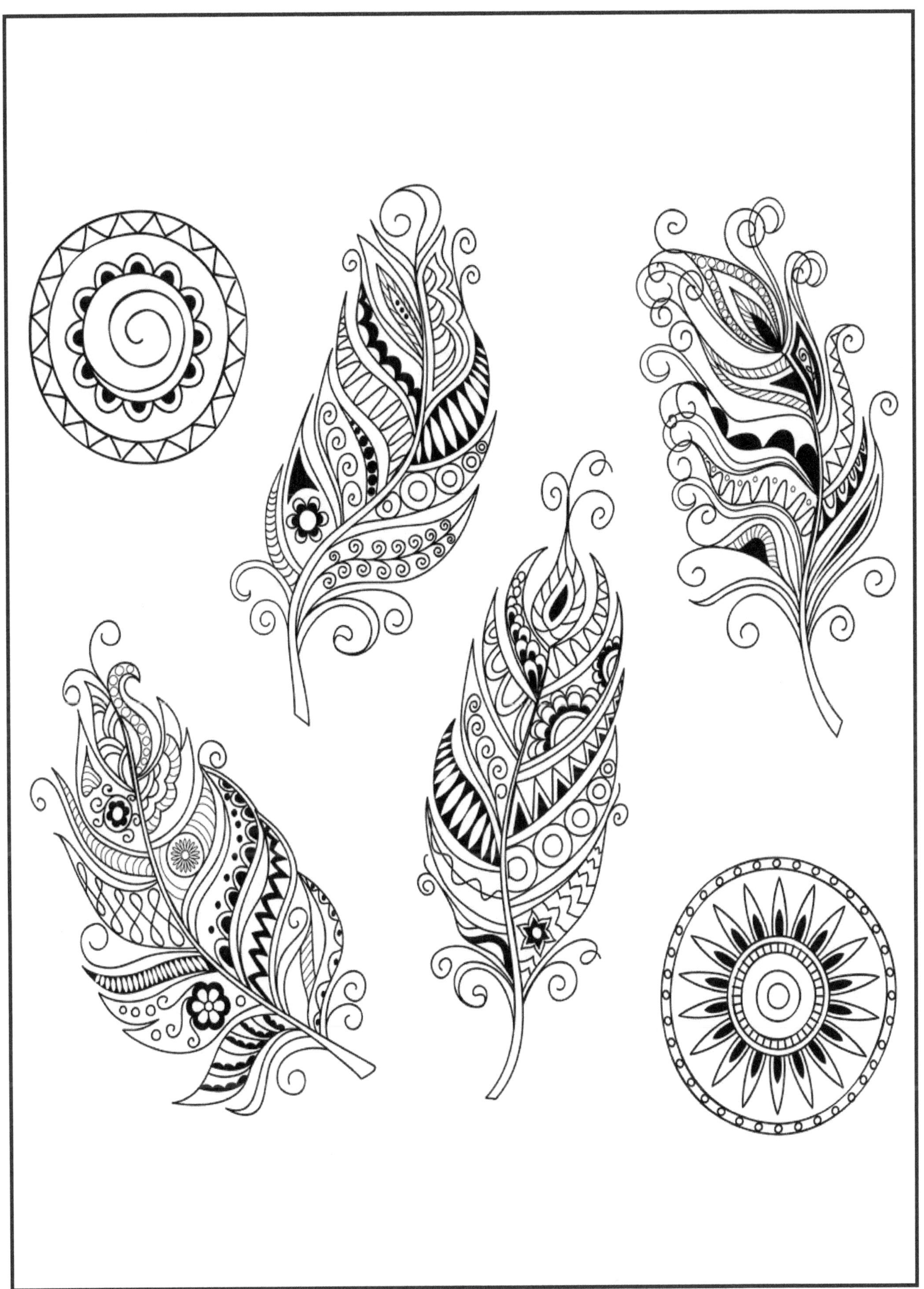

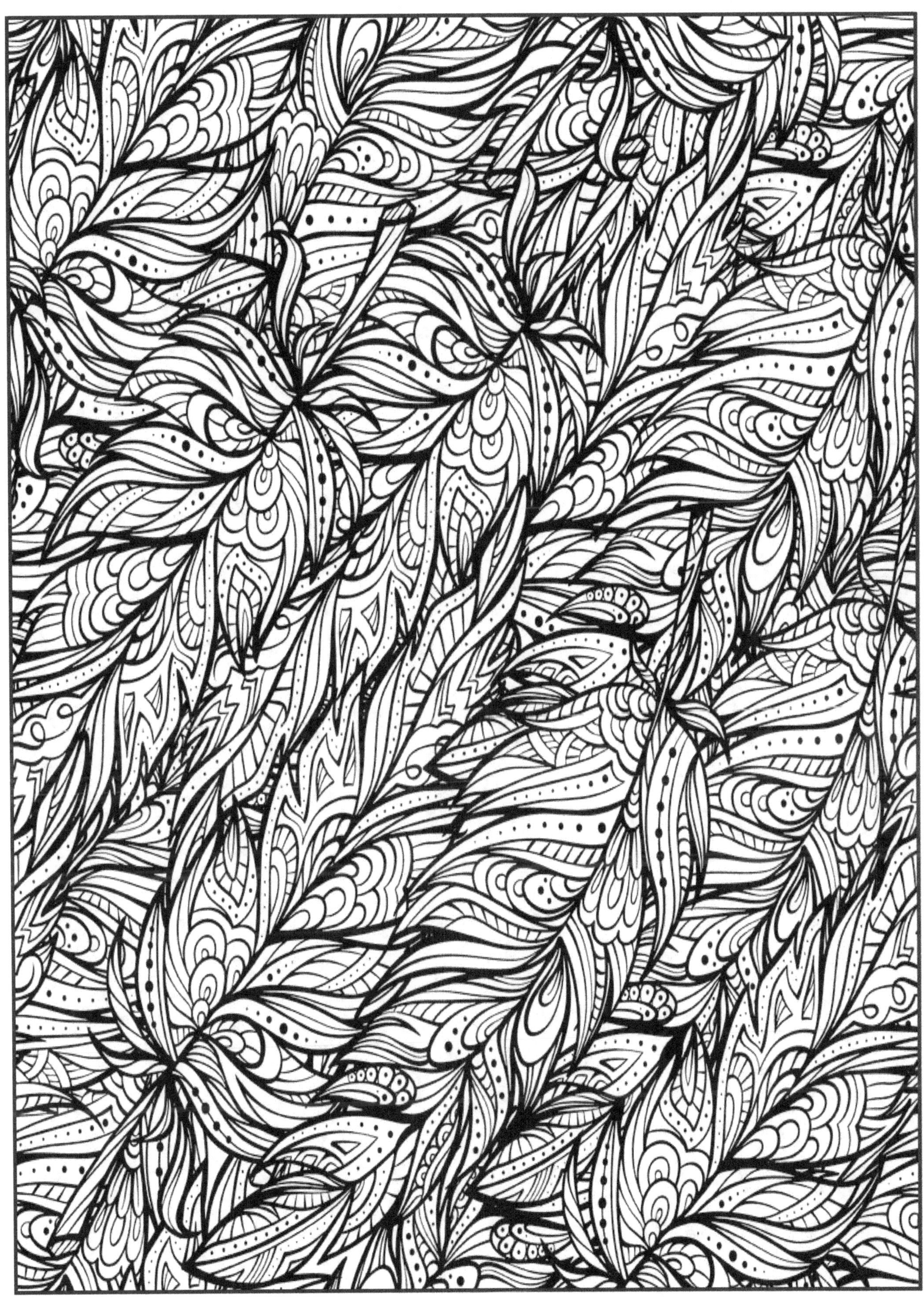

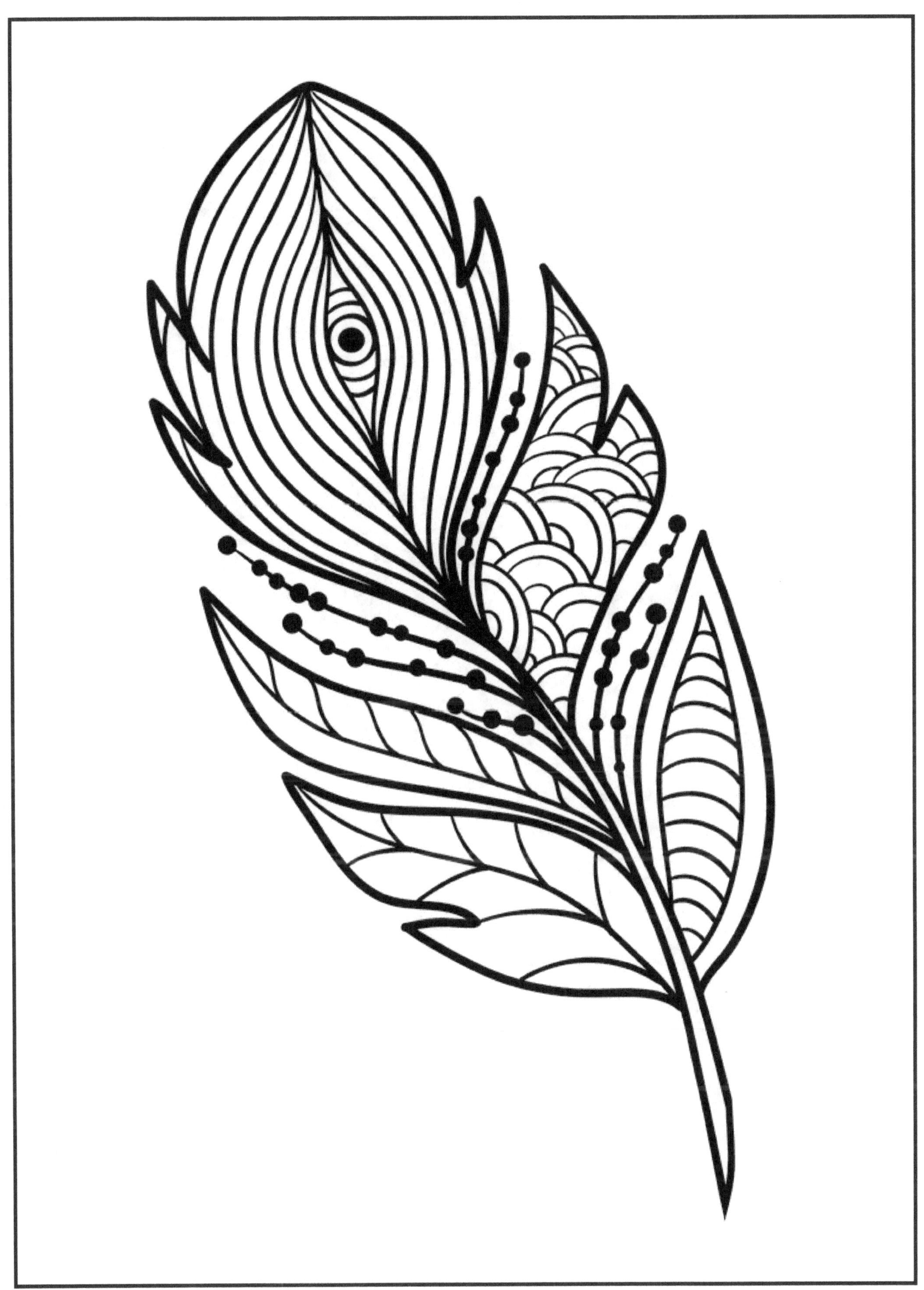

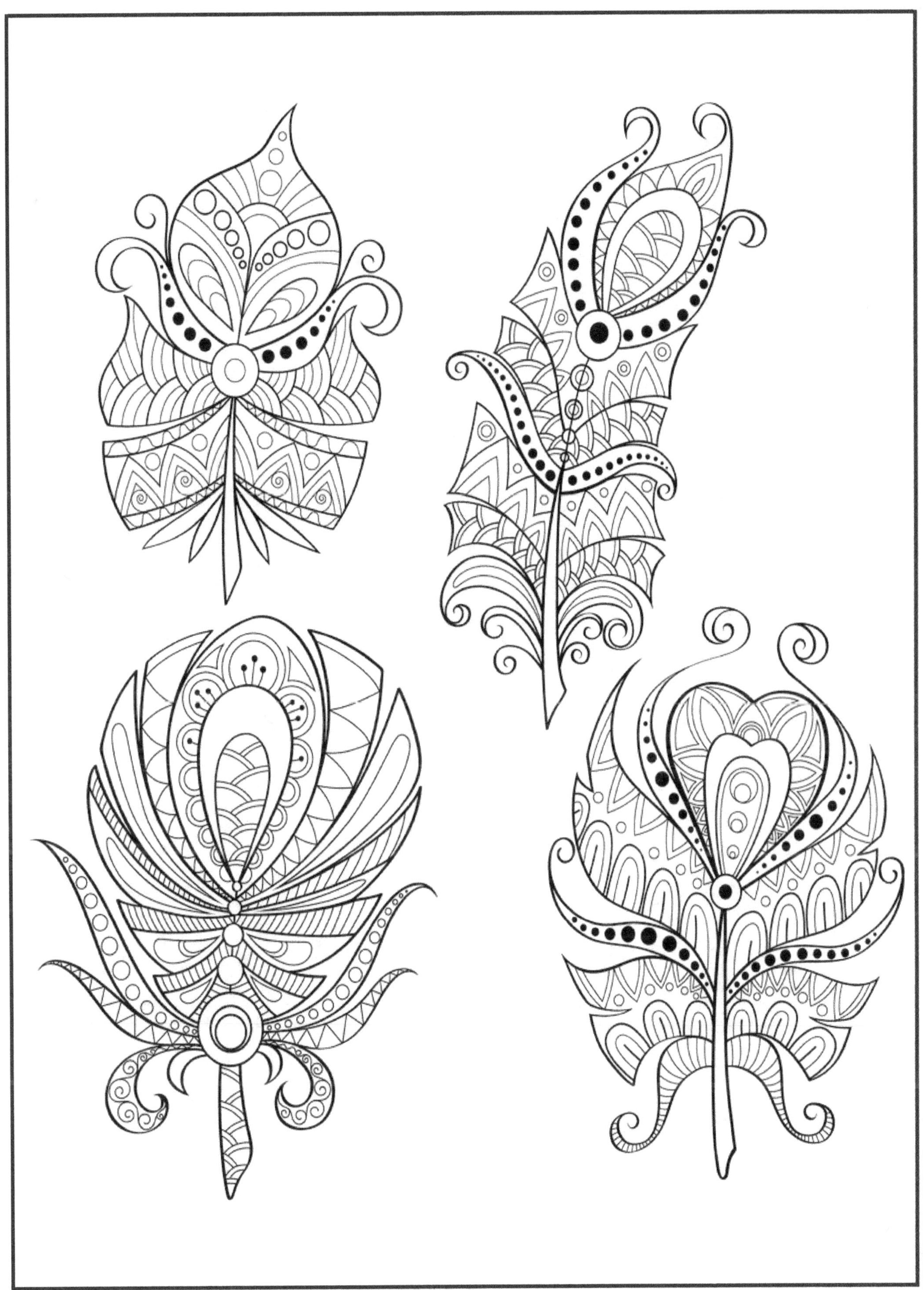

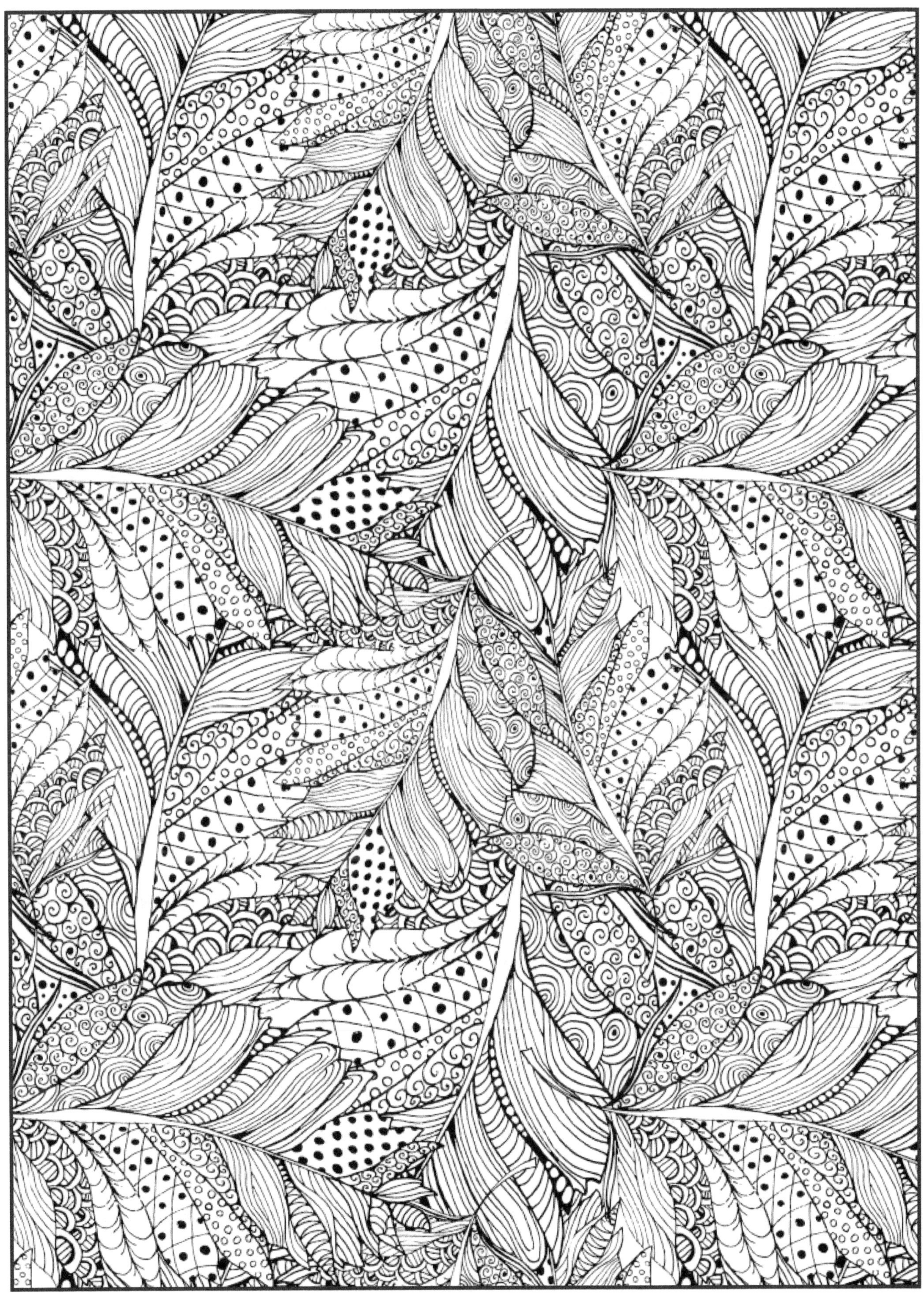

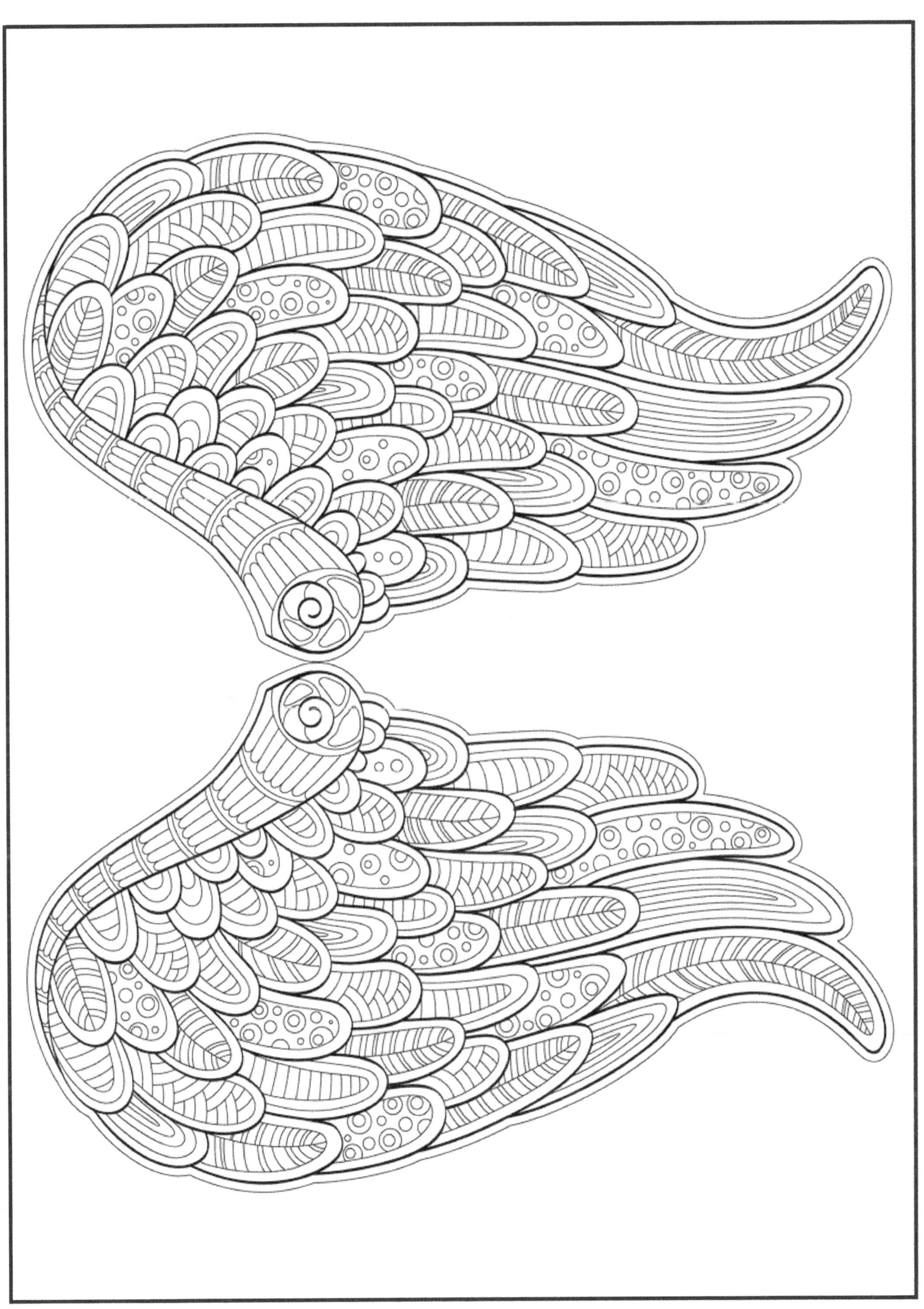

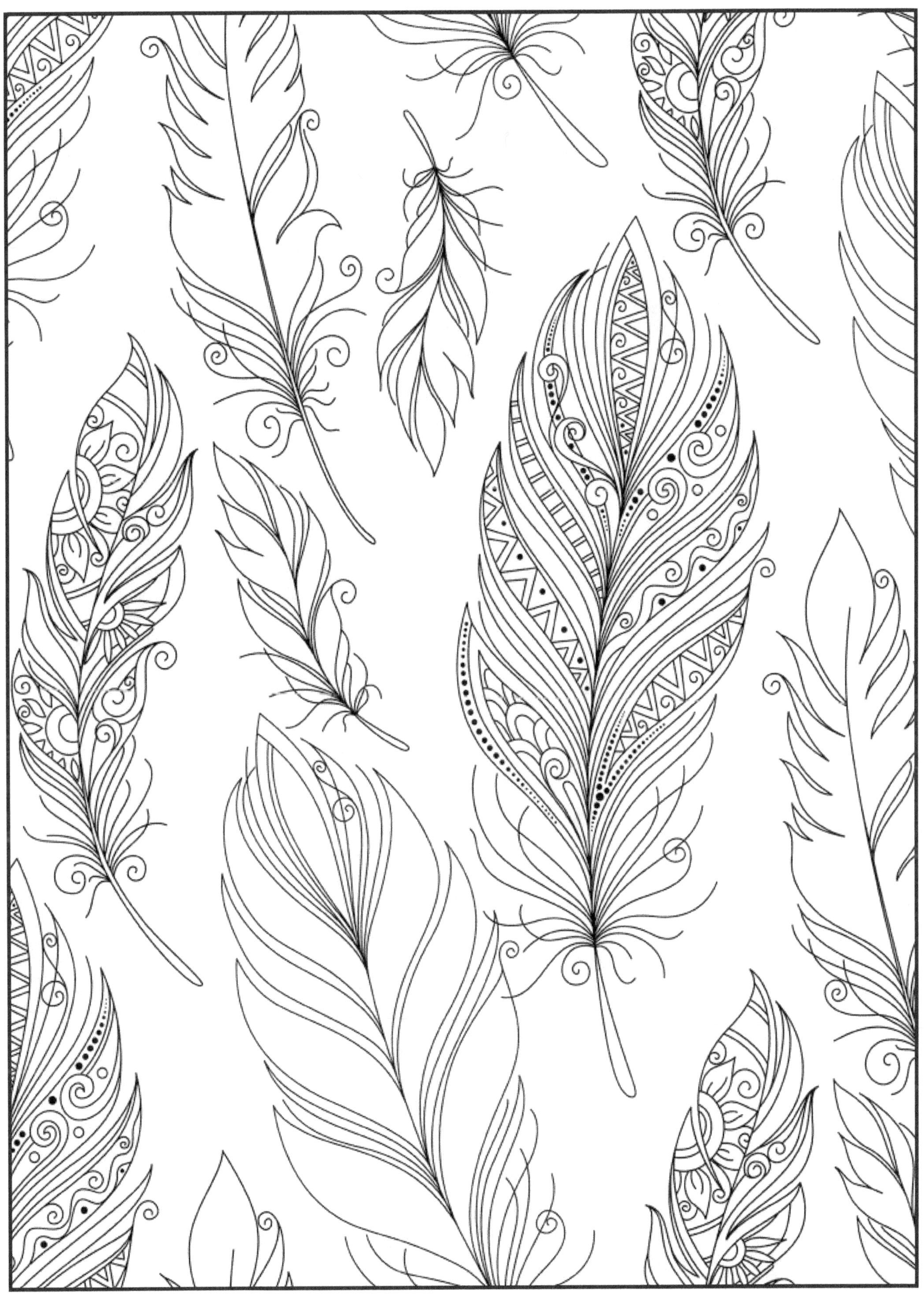

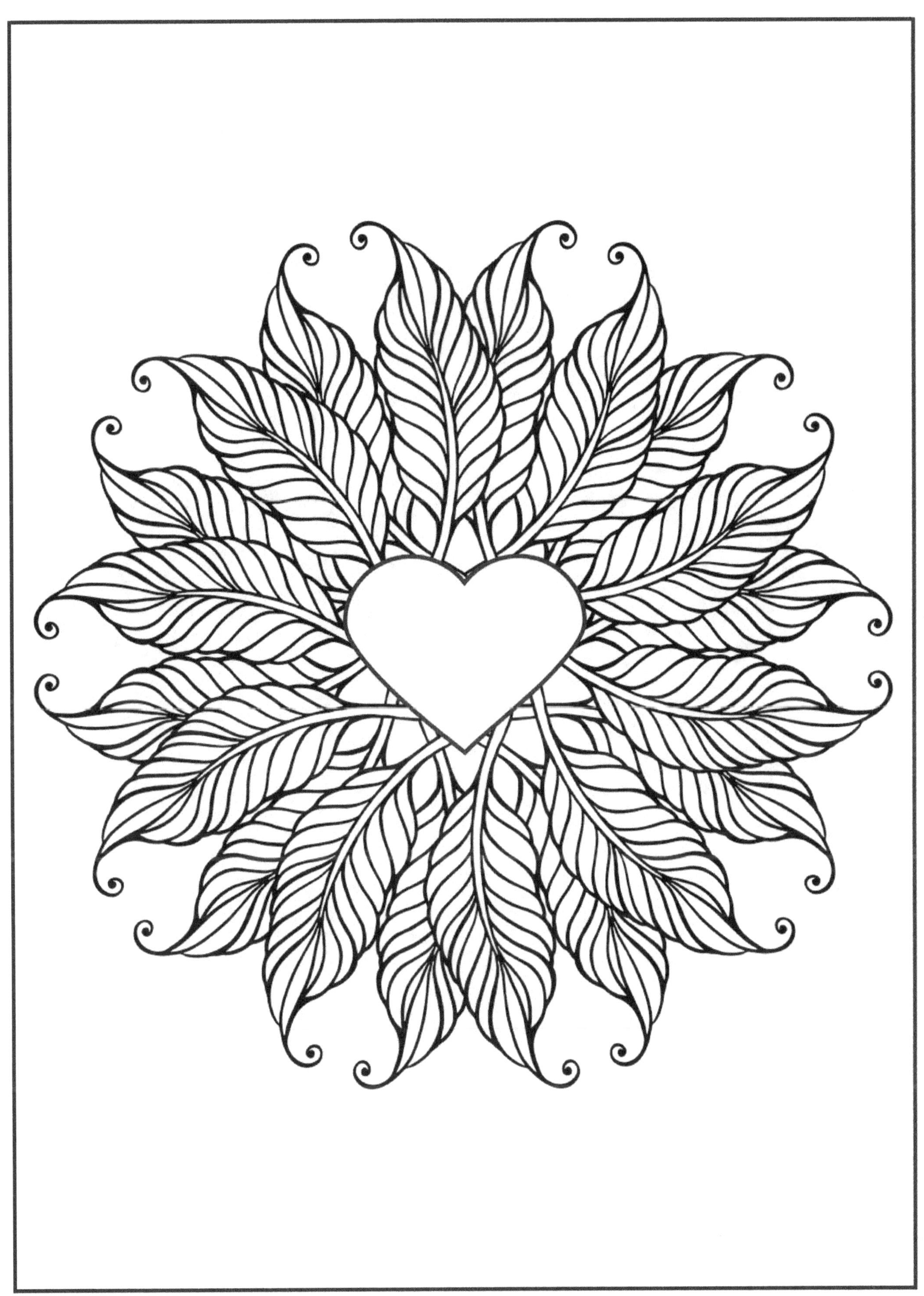

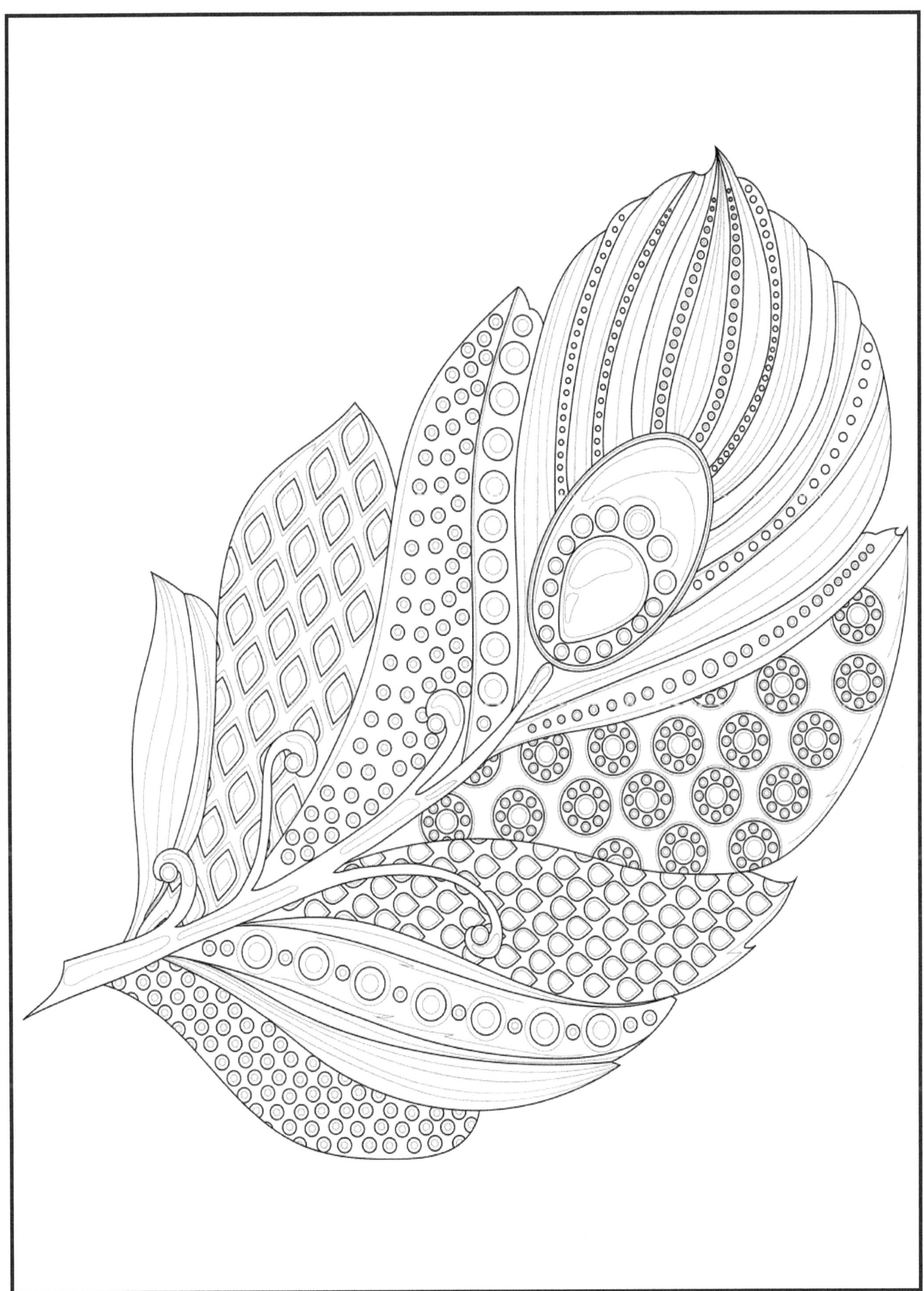

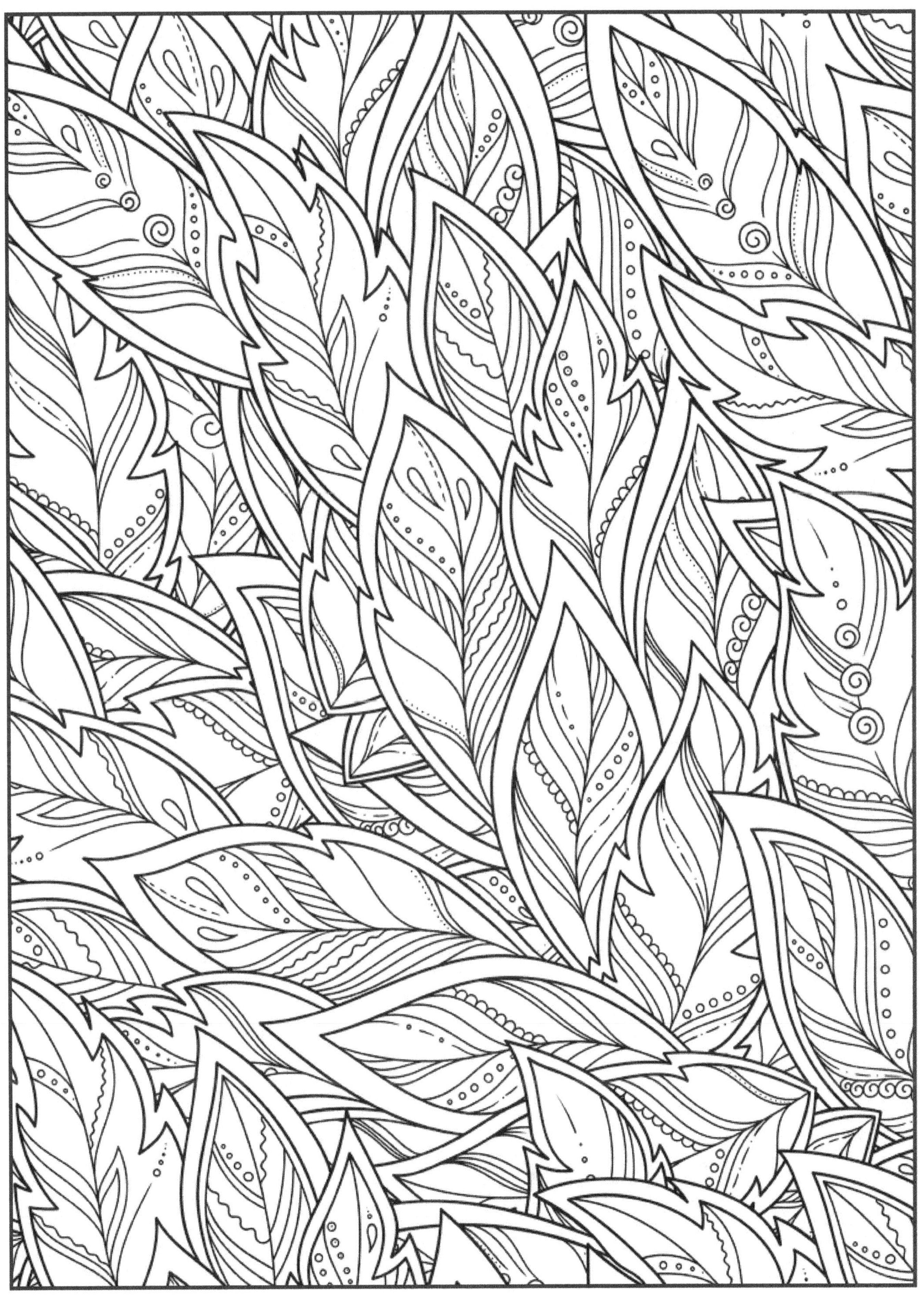

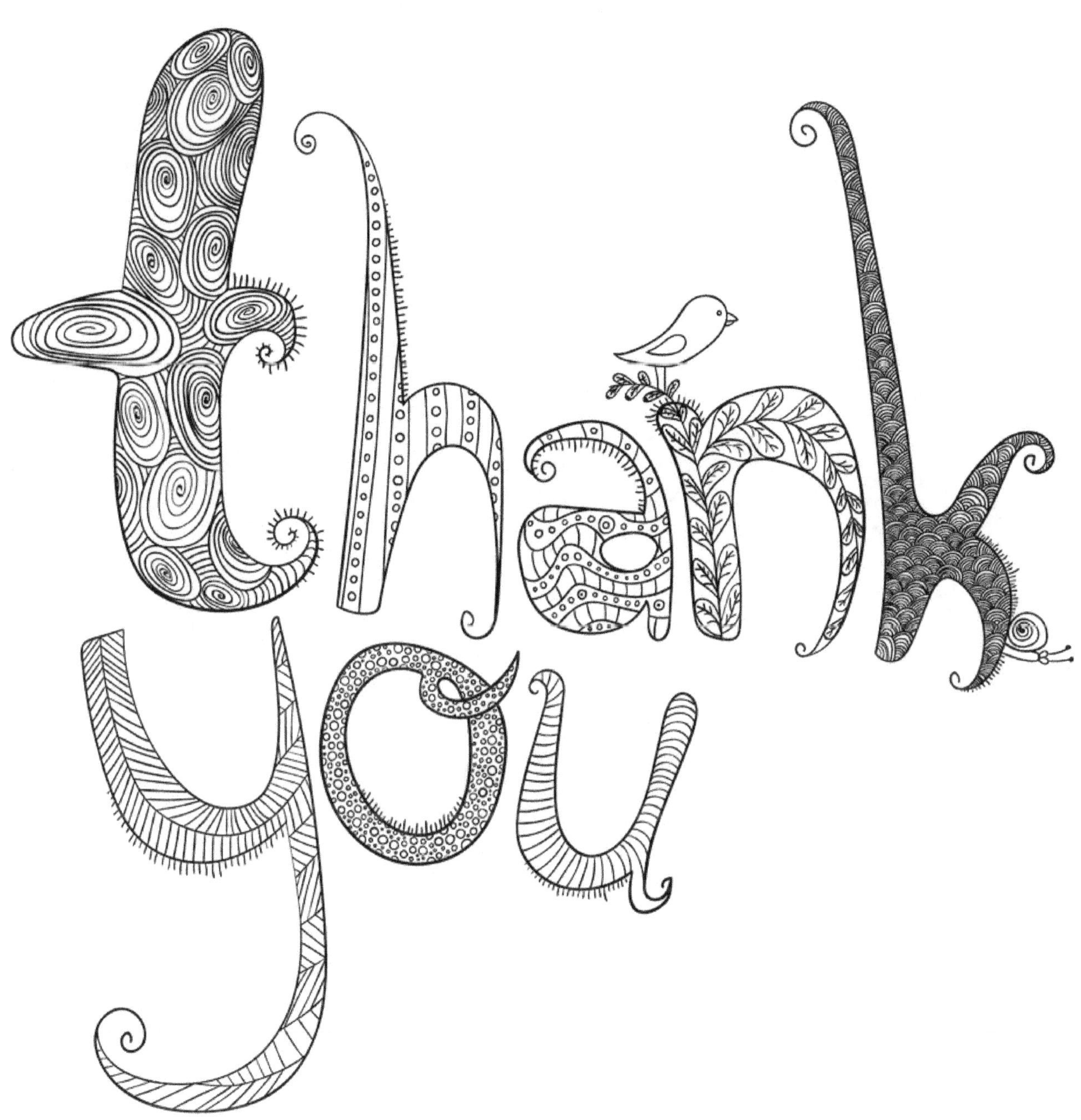